Children, Courts and Caring

Donald Ford

Children, Courts and Caring

A Study of
the Children and Young Persons Act, 1969

Constable London

First published in Great Britain 1975
by Constable and Company Limited
10 Orange Street London WC2H 7EG
Copyright © 1975 by Donald Ford

Hardback ISBN 0 09 460210 7
Paperback ISBN 0 09 460730 3

Set in Monotype Times
Printed in Great Britain by
Ebenezer Baylis and Son Limited
The Trinity Press
Worcester, and London

This book is dedicated with a deep
sense of gratitude to

Paul Cadbury and Anthony Wilson

Foreword

By way of explanation and apology
Lacking scholarship, academic respectability and reputation,
can claim only deep involvement and personal commitment as
justification for writing this book. I offer whatever apologies are
necessary.

Since 1948 I have been concerned in one way or another with
some young people in the process of growing up, and with some
of those trying to help them.

This book is about that experience and as much of the experience of others as I was able to enter into and understand.

Most of my contact with children at risk has been in practical
settings, as Chairman of a Children's Committee and as a
Juvenile Court Magistrate. Neither of these is, in itself, very
satisfactory, but it has given me the opportunity to enter into some
part of the lives of those I write about, even though at all times I
knew I was an intruder.

This is not a distanced, scholarly view, and therefore probably
lacks balance. It is concrete in that it turns to situations with
which I have been concerned, and I accept the dangers and
limitations of that involvement.

I had to adopt such a method because I am more able to handle
specific events and less to deal with large, generalised theories,
about many of which I find I remain sceptical.

Certain theories and views have been enlightening and given
some insight into particular situations. I will inevitably find
myself making generalisations—I am as weak as the next, given
the temptation—but they must be read with all the caveats in
mind.

I hope I can bring something fresh to an urgent discussion
because of the particular blend of experience that I have known.

I would like to express my thanks to all those who have talked
with me and advised me on various parts of the book, and
especially my colleagues in the Inner London Juvenile Courts,
which include the clerks to those courts.

I owe an obvious debt to all the social workers and probation officers who have worked alongside me for many years.

I have a special debt of gratitude to Miss Elfreda Powell of Constable, for her skill and kindness in preparing this work for the press.

All the errors are my own.

My greatest debt is acknowledged in the dedication.

Bushwood 1975   D.F.

Contents

Contents

1

History of Legislation for Children at Risk

The Children and Young Persons Act, 1969, is the latest in a series of such Acts, all of which have been passed in this century. It is important not only for its bearing on the fate of children who come into conflict with society and the law, but also because it brings to a critical point the conflicts centred around our society's attitudes to young people, and the ambiguities and uncertainties in our attitudes to offenders.

The Act was intended to prevent increasing numbers of children coming into court; it sought to make the treatment of youngsters who found themselves in conflict with the law more flexible and responsive than in the past. It significantly changed the emphasis from the 'offence' to the 'offender'.

It also marked a further bold step in the development of community responsibility for those in need and at risk amongst us—a process which has grown apace in the last generation. The emphasis on trying to cope with those in need *within* the community rather than in specialist institutions shut off from the community was extended much more widely to young offenders. It forms part of a wider attempt to retain old people, the mentally ill, the handicapped and inadequate, and the offender within the community, as far as is practicable. This demands of the community a much greater involvement in the lives of their members who, for one reason or another, slip out of the mainstream or come into conflict with the norms prevailing in society.

It is a commonplace to observe that the fate of a child depends very often on whether he or she first bumps into a policeman or a social worker. The Act seeks to reduce the odds in this strange lottery. This aspect of the working of the law and our social provision is not confined to children; there still remains a great element of chance for those of all ages.

The 1969 Act is the most influential Act affecting the law relating to children of the post-war period. It is only exceeded in importance, possibly, by the Children & Young Persons Act of

1933. The consequences of the 1969 Act, if the aspirations which underlie it are achieved, will be more far-reaching than any previous Act, and will ultimately embody a fundamental reappraisal of attitudes to non-conformist behaviour in the young and other sections of our society.

The 1933 Act itself marked a turning point in the law in Section 44:

> Every court, in dealing with a child or young person who is brought before it, either as an offender or otherwise, shall have regard to the welfare of the child or young person and shall in a proper case take steps for removing him from undesirable surroundings, or for securing that proper provision is made for his education and training.

Since we have lived with this idea for many years, it has become part of our thinking and it may not seem much of an advance today. In its time it was revolutionary in directing attention to the needs of the child.

The change, however, between the attitude revealed in that quotation and the 1969 Act is best demonstrated by a quotation from the White Paper, *Children in Trouble*, which preceded the Act.

> A child's behaviour is influenced by genetic, emotional and intellectual factors, his maturity and his family, school, neighbourhood and wider social setting. It is probably a minority of children who grow up in ways which may be contrary to the law. Frequently such behaviour is no more than an incident in the pattern of a child's normal development. But sometimes it is a response to unsatisfactory family or social circumstances, a result of boredom in and out of school, an indication of maladjustment or immaturity, or a symptom of a deviant, damaged or abnormal personality. Early recognition and full assessment are particularly important in these more serious cases. Variety and flexibility in the measures that can be taken are equally important, if society is to deal effectively and appropriately with these manifold aspects of delinquency. The measures include supervision and support of the child in the family: the further development of the services working in the community:

and a variety of facilities for short-term and long-term care, treatment and control, including some which are highly specialised.

The change of emphasis is striking. In 1933 the main emphasis lay on removing the child from undesirable or unfavourable surroundings. In 1969 the emphasis is on keeping the child in the community where possible, and working with the child in that context. The insistence on the need for co-ordinated work on many levels is also important. The fact that the child is looked at less as an individual and more as part of a background of family, of other social groupings and of the community reflects the practical experience of many years of work and thought since 1933.

It also stresses that the decision to remove a child from the community is one which can only be arrived at when many factors extraneous to the child and any possible offences have been taken into account, and should only be contemplated in the light of the fullest information and the most careful scrutiny and consideration. It was this aspect which aroused the greatest outcry from certain of the juvenile court magistrates. In effect it took away from the magistrates the right to decide whether a child should remain within the community, or be removed from home and inserted into an artificial community. Many magistrates, apparently, found this deprivation hard to bear.

Despite the difference in emphasis the 1969 Act can be seen as the logical successor to the Act of 1933. The earlier Act was important for a number of reasons. It was the first time that the law recognised that there was a group of children in trouble who were not readily amenable to the criminal law. It extended the concept of welfare to the child who came within the purview of the criminal law, and it directed attention to the child's needs in social terms and introduced a concept of welfare to set against earlier concepts of punishment.

At the time, though many recognised the quality of the departure from the past, the act caused much controversy, and for a number of years there was an outcry against it, ascribing increases in crime to its provisions. The 1969 Act, although so far only implemented in part, has aroused similar reactions; it was designed to make a further, even more fundamental break with the past. Those who have now come to love the old Act, execrate the new.

The passage of the Act to the statute book illustrates many of the difficulties which confronted those who sought change. The Bill was preceded by two White Papers. The first, entitled *The Child, the Family and the Young Offender*, was issued in August 1965 by the Home Office, and its stated purpose was to 'invite discussion of possible measures to support the family, forestall and prevent delinquency and revise the law and practice relating to young offenders in England and Wales'.

The invitation was taken up with alacrity. There was a great deal of serious discussion and detailed debate, and many contrary views were expressed, but much of the discourse deteriorated into cries of alarm and outrage from many different directions and interest groups. Nearly three years later, in April 1968, a second White Paper, *Children in Trouble*, was published. The proposals in this second paper had been considerably modified, possibly in the light of experience after the intensity of the reaction to its predecessor. Nevertheless it retained its emphasis on constructive, preventive work in an effort to reduce the number of children coming into conflict with the law or appearing before a court.

The White Paper, *The Child, the Family and the Young Offender*, set out proposals for practical reforms to support the family group, prevent and reduce delinquency, and to create new practices in administering the law for offenders up to the age of twenty-one.

It proposed a Family Service, coupled with Family Councils. These councils were intended largely to supersede the juvenile courts. The process suggested for dealing with young offenders was as follows: The symptoms of trouble in the child or young person's life would be presented through an allegation that an offence had been committed, or that the child or young person was in need of care, protection or control, or failing to attend school or work. These facts would be reported to the Family Council. The necessary enquiries would then follow, and the Council would then see the parents and child. It was felt that in most cases the facts, once established, would be agreed. If agreement were reached the Council would proceed to devise ways of helping the child.

In some cases it would be clear that the parents could themselves deal adequately with the situation. In others it might be disposed of by the parents paying compensation to anyone who had suffered loss from the child's delinquency. In yet other cases, agreement might be reached on the desirability of placing the child under the supervision of an officer of the children's service, or of sending him for some form of residential training. Any agreement thus reached would be formally recorded. It could be varied from time to time in agreement with the parents: and the case would, in any event, be reviewed from year to year.

If there was failure to agree on the facts, the case would stand referred to the Family Court, which would hear the facts, and then return the case to the Family Council for discussion of treatment, if it felt, on the basis of these facts, that some consideration of treatment was indicated. A case would also be referred to the Family Court if an agreement about treatment were not complied with. The Family Court would, in effect, be the present juvenile court, at one remove, with much limited functions, particularly as to disposal.

At this juncture, I would like to interpolate my personal reactions as a juvenile magistrate to indicate some of the points for and against the proposals as they were set out.

I wholeheartedly supported the intentions underlying the proposals, but I was not happy about the machinery which was proposed.

The whole process of working with children in trouble depends in large part on the consent of the youngster and the family, where that can be won. Even within the context of a juvenile court the first aim is to win that consent. It is not always possible because the necessary action is not palatable in the short term, but a degree of good will can usually be won from parents and child.

But that consent can be assumed too easily on occasions. There is a desire of many parents 'to get it over with'. Consent can be obtained by acquiescence to pressure, through fear of what consequences may follow a refusal to co-operate. Many times a court is faced with parents who want a child to plead guilty to an offence, so that an action can be concluded with dispatch. If this can happen in the court setting, where legal advice is readily available, how much greater is the danger in the context of a Family Council?

There is no answer to this question in the Welsh and English system, since, in the end, the Family Councils did not come into being. However, a similar solution became law in Scotland, and my discussions with a number of those involved in the Scottish system shows that some part of that unease was justified.

The parents of a proportion of children in trouble are often inadequate or lacking in responsibility, confused or highly ashamed; they have little idea of where to turn for help and advice, and little energy or inclination to seek help or assert such rights. The Family Council, working especially with such parents, would not be subject to scrutiny. The whole process would create a marked increase in bureaucratic power; certain matters which were, and have continued to be, handled judicially, with all the law's imperfections and shortcomings, would be dealt with by an administrative machine, less accessible to challenge, more opaque to scrutiny, with none of the safeguards that the court, with all its deficiencies, provides.

In the end I came down, marginally, against the idea of a Family Council because I felt that the rights of the child and the parents were better safeguarded by some form of judicial procedure in the first instance, before considerations of treatment and intervention in the lives of children and their families were allowed.

Many of those who claim to be defending the rights of the individual are too often, unfortunately, defending their own right to punish. I hope I do not fall into that category. My own view, at least consciously, is that the liberty of a child is no less important than the liberty of any other citizen. Age is no consideration. The intervention of any outside agent in the life of a child or the child's family is as great an infringement of the liberty of the child as it is of any other person, and this in despite of the benevolent intention or manifest good-will of the intervening agent. I know that if this view is pushed to extremes many anomalies appear, and do in any practical situation at present. I felt that this was one area of advance that should be looked at hard.

The court, in effect, is the licenser of such intervention; it is good that the issuing of the licence is removed from the agencies seeking to intervene, and that the process allows the court to submit those agencies to a degree of scrutiny. My own view, simply, was that the right to intervene should be tested first.

On that basis, and it was agonisingly marginal, I came to the conclusion that the juvenile court, in a modified form, should

survive with a useful function, but that the decisions as to subsequent treatment should more properly pass to those who were
trained and had the necessary skills to take such decisions. This
was much more the view of the second White Paper, *Children in
Trouble,* which resulted in the 1969 Act.

The 1969 Act is the culmination of the establishment of a body
of law and practice in respect of children which is of compara-
tively recent development (except with regard to property); the
major legislation coming entirely within this century. Each stage
of the development has been marked by fierce controversy.

Until 1847 the law did not discriminate between children and
other offenders; it prided itself on its impartiality, despite the
fact that, in practice, it had used criteria other than age, to make
such discriminations. If children or young persons were charged
with an indictable offence they had the right to trial by jury at an
Assizes or Quarter Sessions; for non-indictable offences (these
are usually but not invariably less serious) they were tried summarily before magistrates along with all other offenders.

They were also subject to the full range of the penalties of the
law, once any offence had been proved against them. They were
hanged for theft in the name of impartiality, along with others
older than themselves. In the eighteenth century, nine out of ten
of those hanged were under the age of twenty-one. Those who
escaped hanging were sent to serve their sentences in prisons
where conditions were harsh, brutal, brutalising and corrupting.
The same rigours applied to these youngsters on arrest, even if
subsequently they were found innocent. Many of the reformers of
the day thought that this experience was sufficiently corrosive to
blight a child for ever.

In the days when transportation was an accepted form of
punishment it was often used for young offenders to avoid hanging
them. In 1831 the Superintendent of the Hulks, in which the
youngsters lay along with all other prisoners while awaiting their
journey overseas, gave evidence to the fact that the youngest of
his charges was 'nine years old and deemed incorrigible'. We
cannot judge of this child today, but it is important to remember
that no sentence of transportation could be carried out until the
convict was fourteen, so that this child, along with hundreds of
others, would wait for years before being shipped out.

This was the sort of scandal which possibly made those who
were despatched more speedily by the rope recipients of more

mercy than they might have appreciated. The fate of these children and many thousands more like them had been cause for concern for a long time. Two of the best known and influential figures who had tried to do something in this field were the novelist, Henry Fielding, and his brother, 'The Blind Beak', both of whom served as the magistrate at Bow Street.

They did all they could to further the interests of the Philanthropic Society, which had founded an institution at Redhill, much changed but still existing today. A number of other philanthropic organisations and religious bodies did what they could in the light of their conscience and predilections by founding institutions for the care and training of children, but the law did not recognise any distinction between children and other offenders.

In 1817 the *Second Report of the House of Commons Committee on the State of the Police in the Metropolis* gave, as an incidental intelligence, the interesting statistic that the newly opened prison at Clerkenwell had received 399 convicted felons aged from 9 to 19 in one year. Many of those so incarcerated were flogged on admission and discharge, and then 'without a shilling in their pockets, turned loose upon the world more hardened in character than ever', even if their backs, for a brief spell, were more tender.

No separate provision for the detention of young offenders was made until 1838 when Parkhurst, still with us today as a prison for adults, was converted from a military hospital to a prison for the reception of young offenders up to the age of eighteen. This followed upon the report of a Select Committee of the House of Lords set up to enquire into the state of gaols and prisons which had been sitting since 1835.

As a result of the representation of various reformers the Act of 1847 allowed offenders charged with stealing to be tried summarily in a Magistrates' Court, thus removing children from the full rigours of the law, since the powers of the lower court were less extensive. This reform was introduced because of concern at the lack of convictions for theft; plaintiffs were refusing to prosecute children and youngsters because of the penalties they were liable to upon conviction.

One such active campaigner was Mary Carpenter, who attacked the Parkhurst system in a book published in 1851. The title of her work, *Reformatory Schools for the Children of the Perishing and Dangerous Classes and for Juvenile Offenders*, reflects rather quaintly some of the preconceptions of the day. The arrangements at Parkhurst, insofar as they provided for the separation of young offenders from the mass of convicts, were an advance, but the régime was harsh. Mary Carpenter indicted Parkhurst for its repressive régime and brutal discipline, for its lack of corrective and constructive work, and revealed that the guards were armed, the prisoners shackled and the whip in frequent use.

Her view was that the State should not be involved in the provision of institutions for children and young offenders; she preferred a series of Reformatories run on the lines of the Industrial Schools and Orphan Homes which had been established by various religious bodies and charitable organisations. Government control, in that epoch, meant central government control; there was no local government machinery capable of assuming responsibility for such provisions.

The Youthful Offenders Act, 1854, authorised the setting up of Reformatory Schools, which were to be organised by voluntary societies, subject to the inspection and approval of the Home Office. The young offenders, however, had to spend a period in prison, before being sent on to such an institution. Parkhurst ceased to be a boys' prison in 1864.

The Summary Jurisdiction Act of 1879 enlarged the provision of the Act of 1847, so that offenders under the age of sixteen could be tried summarily for nearly all indictable offences. These measures were beneficial in two directions: they reduced the numbers of juveniles held in prisons and they simplified the trial process for young offenders. In practice they reduced the penalties to which young offenders were subject. Nevertheless many children still found their way to prison along with adult offenders (a few still do so today!), and juveniles were still tried in the ordinary courts along with adults.

The next advance did not come until the great wave of reform initiated by the Liberal Government in the 1900s. A series of Acts reflected changed attitudes in this field. The first was the Probation Act of 1907, which 'nationalised' the work of the Court Missionaries—pioneering work undertaken by the churches. The Children Act, 1908, and the Prevention of Crime Act followed. The Children Act laid down, for the first time, the principle that young offenders should be treated entirely separately from adults and established the Juvenile Courts.

Offenders under the age of sixteen had to be tried in a juvenile court, except under very exceptional circumstances, the principal exception being if a child had been involved in committing an offence with an adult.

The Juvenile Court was a court of summary jurisdiction, but it was decreed that it had to sit in a different place or at a different time from the ordinary court. This was intended to protect the child from associating with older offenders, professional criminals, drunks and some other less desirable people.

Imprisonment of children under fourteen was abolished, and those aged between fourteen and sixteen were subject to imprisonment only under exceptional circumstances: the conditions laid down were such that for practical purposes the matter ceased to be an issue.

The emphasis in the treatment of children moved away from punishment and towards reformation. The Act allowed a degree of 'welfare concern' into the treatment of children in the court. This, in association with the new Probation Act, and experience gained from the working of that Act, created a new approach to the problems of the youthful offender. The Crime Prevention Act of the same year created specialised detention for young offenders, known as Borstal detention (later called Borstal training) from the name of the village where the first institution was set up.

The constitution of the juvenile courts remained the same, however, and the justices who sat in what may now be called the adult courts also sat in the juvenile courts. It was not until an Act of 1920, affecting the London County Council area only, that a specially selected panel of magistrates was created to hear cases in the juvenile courts of the metropolis. The chairman of the court was a Metropolitan Stipendiary Magistrate, sitting with two lay justices, one of whom had to be a woman. This panel was appointed by the Home Secretary, on advice, and was supposed to be constituted of people of special suitability for service of this kind.

This practice was adopted for the whole country in the Children and Young Persons Act, 1933. The justices in each area were empowered to create a panel from amongst their number to sit in the juvenile courts; they also appointed their chairmen from the lay justices.

Ironically the London juvenile courts did not sit under lay chairmen until 1936, when, as a result of a further special act, they were brought more or less into line with the rest of the country. The anomaly still remains, however, as a hangover from the past, that the chairmen of the juvenile courts in London are appointed by the Lord Chancellor, while the stipendiary magistrates still occasionally take the chair in some of the Inner London Juvenile Courts, and also join with the chairmen in various meetings.

The Children and Young Persons Act of 1933, as previously mentioned, is the great watershed in this field of legislation. It laid down clearly and unequivocally that welfare was to be the principal consideration in dealing with juveniles. This principle had first been enunciated in the Guardianship of Infants Act, 1925: 'Where in any proceedings before any court . . . the custody or upbringing of an infant . . . is in question, the court, in deciding the question, shall regard the welfare of the infant as the first and paramount consideration.'

In Section 44 of the 1933 Act, quoted earlier, this consideration was widened in respect of age and to include those who were in conflict with the law. This was taken a great deal further in various Acts after 1933 and culminated in the Act of 1969. It demonstrates an interesting phenomenon of the law: very often provision made exceptionally for a small minority of special vulnerability or concern can gradually be extended to apply to much larger numbers and wider categories. Much of the discrimination and special provision made initially in respect of age since the Act of 1847 has led to the development of practices which have percolated through the law to affect other and much wider groups.

It is for this reason that what happened in the juvenile courts after 1933 was of importance eventually in a much broader field of legislation; it opened the way for developments in the judicial process and thinking which were relevant to people other than children and young persons. For the same reason what has happened as a result of the 1969 Act is of importance not only for the age groups immediately affected but for the whole shape and future practice of the law and penal policy.

2

The Provisions of the 1969 Act

Between the Children and Young Persons Act of 1933 and that of 1969 came a similarly entitled Act: the Children and Young Persons Act of 1963. This was based on the recommendations of the Ingleby Committee, and it modified many of the provisions of the 1933 Act.

The Ingleby Committee focused their attention on the child as a member of the family and community. It stated:

The child cannot be regarded as an isolated unit. The problem is always one of the child in his environment and his immediate environment is the family to which he belongs. It is the situation and the relationships with the family which seem to be responsible for many children being in trouble, whether the trouble is called delinquency or anything else. It is often parents who need to alter their ways, and it is therefore with family troubles that any preventive measures will be concerned.

The emphasis on preventive measures was the most important single achievement of the Committee and the Act. The involvement of the parents was ensured by stating that wherever possible, both parents of a child should be required to attend court with the child. Also emphasised was the need to discuss and explain fully to the child and the parents the measures that the court had under consideration.

To take a view of the child against the background of family, home and community, rather than in stark isolation with his detected wrongdoing, was fruitful in its consequences. These insights, already familiar to various social workers, brought the problems into a new focus for the rest of the community.

To further the work of prevention, much greater co-ordination of the various agencies at work in the field became desirable. The recommendations of the Committee and the Act enlarged the statutory scope of social work considerably.

Prior to this report the statutory provision had been sharply delineated and highly particularised, addressed to certain specific areas of concern. This arose partially from the pattern of local government and the piecemeal way in which solutions for particular problems had been devised in the past.

Certain categories of people, with physical or mental illness, physical or mental handicaps, or those showing problems of maladjustment or delinquency or inadequacy were the chief recipients of concern. The committee compelled a much wider-ranging look at the problems and forced a recognition of their many dimensions; it was not able to cut through the jungle of interlocking departmental divisions and jealousies, but it did highlight the need for such surgery. This was a fruitful opening which led to much more dramatic developments in a relatively short time; the Ingleby Committee prepared the way not only for the 1963 Act, but also for the Act of 1969.

There would have been no 1969 Act without the interim provision of the act of 1963; the success of the Ingleby Committee can, in fact, be judged from the short period which elapsed between the two Acts.

Certain specific recommendations were adopted. The Ingleby Committee recommended the raising of the age of criminal responsibility from eight years to twelve, with a subsequent adjustment to the age of 13 or 14. The Act was framed more timorously, and raised the limit to ten.

To cope with children under the age of criminal responsibility who were 'in trouble of some sort' a new procedure was recommended. The old 'in need of care and protection' provision of the 1933 Act was dispensed with, as was the provision which made it possible for a parent to bring one of the children of the family before the court as being 'beyond control'. This was done to prevent the terrifying rejection implicit in a process where the parent became the chief accuser and had to make a case against his own child in a court of law.

Various other changes were made in the law, but since for the most part they were modified subsequently or taken further by the 1969 Act, it is probably better to pass to the provisions of the later Act to avoid confusion.

Nevertheless it is important to bear in mind the passing of the 1963 Act; it led on inevitably to the later Act and it opened the door to rapid and considerable change.

The 1969 Act sets out the tests for taking what are called 'care proceedings' in the juvenile court in Section 1 of the Act.

The court must be satisfied:

1. That the child's development is being avoidably prevented or neglected, or his health is being avoidably impaired or neglected, or he is being ill-treated;

OR

2. That similar conditions as indicated above have been proved in respect of another child in the same household;

OR

3. He is exposed to moral danger;

OR

4. He is beyond the control of his parent or guardian;

OR

5. He is truanting when of compulsory school age;

OR

6. He is guilty of an offence in law, excluding homicide;

AND ALSO

That he is in need of care or control which he is unlikely to receive unless the court makes an order in respect of him.

The last requirement must be satisfied along with any of the others which precede it. This last requirement is described by many social workers as a 'trip-wire' on the route to court; it is designed to prevent as many children as possible from being brought to court.

There are, in fact, two such 'trip-wires'. Section 4 of the Act states that 'a person shall not be charged with an offence except homicide, by reason of anything done while he is a child'. In effect this provision brings the child who is over the age of criminal responsibility (ten years) but under the minimum age for prosecution (fourteen years) within the ambit of civil as opposed to criminal proceedings.

The Act defines clearly those who can bring a child before the court; these include the local authority, a constable or other authorised person. Later it is made clear that the constable or authorised person (for the purposes of the Act the authorised person is an officer of the National Society for the Prevention of Cruelty to Children) may not bring a child before the court unless he is satisfied that only a court order will suffice to help the child in the circumstances in which he finds himself. This in effect places the local authority and the relevant department of that authority, the Social Services Department, at the heart of all decisions on bringing a child to court.

The police or other agency must satisfy themselves that only a court order will suffice, and they must inform the local authority that this is their view; the local authority is free to take a different view, and it must provide the court 'before which proceedings are heard with such information relating to the home surroundings, school record, health and character of the person in respect of whom proceedings are brought as appear to the local authority likely to assist the court'.

This applies for all those who, in the eyes of the law, are children. For those between the ages of fourteen and seventeen there are similar safeguards. The police or any 'qualified informant' (in effect, a local authority official or a member of the transport police) may prosecute for an offence only if he is satisfied 'that it would not be adequate for the case to be dealt with by a parent, teacher or other person or by means of a caution from a constable or through the exercise of the powers of a local authority or other body not involving court proceedings'.

The effect of these qualifications has been to compel much closer liaison between the police and the local authority at a stage prior to the decision to prosecute. Such consultation has become a well-established routine, so that even before prosecution, the child or young person is studied as well as the offence. Even if the prosecution of a young offender were carried through without first consulting the local authority, as is theoretically possible, the court would not be able to deal with the offender even if the case were proved until, as a result of enquiries carried out by the local authority, the views and attitude of the local authority were known.

Most of the large police forces, especially in urban areas, have now established their own separate department, the juvenile bureau, which considers every case before a decision whether or not to prosecute is taken. Because of this, consultation between the police and the local authority Social Services Department has become even closer.

In these ways the net first spread by the 1963 Act to prevent numbers of children coming to court has been cast wider and its meshes made more discriminating. Cautioning of young offenders by the police has been given statutory sanction for the first time. At the same time a young person's right to claim trial by jury has been removed.

These are some of the aspects of bringing a child or young person to court. Other important changes in the Act deal with the powers of the juvenile court in disposing of a case, and these proposals have proved to be the most contentious of all.

In the past the court could make various orders: a Probation Order, a Fit Person Order or an Approved School Order. The Probation Order placed the offender on probation and under the supervision of the probation officer who was an officer of the court. The Fit Person Order placed the child in the care of a 'fit person' usually meaning the Children's Department of the local authority. The Approved School Order was made to remove a child immediately from home and place him, after assessment, in an approved school.

The court had other ways of disposing of a case: the means usually employed for more serious cases. By and large magistrates tended to grade these various forms of disposal. The new provisions simplified the scale. The court now has power to make two orders: a Supervision Order or a Care Order.

The Supervision Order places the child under the supervision of the local authority or the probation service; the Care Order places the child in the care of the local authority, and the authority then has the powers and duties in respect of the child or young person of a parent or guardian.

Basing his view on past experience, the magistrate roughly equated the Supervision Order with the previous Probation Order where the child could be supervised at home. The Care Order, since it allowed the child to be received into a community home or any other institution used to accommodate children or young persons in trouble, was seen as equivalent to the Approved School Order or the Fit Person Order, something to be resorted to in cases presenting more serious problems and giving rise for greater concern.

The difference lay in the fact that the decision as to the placement and treatment of the child was left to the social worker and removed from the court. Many magistrates found this hard to accept.

The full range of orders available to the court in care proceedings are as follows:

1. an order requiring the parent or guardian to enter into an undertaking, backed by a financial penalty, to exercise proper care and control over the youngster;
2. a supervision order;
3. a care order;
4. a hospital order—this procedure is laid down in the Mental Health Act, 1959, and such an order must be supported by two doctors;
5. a guardianship order, which has to have the same support as 4 above.

For young persons, there is a power to bind over the offender for up to £25, for a period of one year, to be of good behaviour; if there is a further breach of the law, that money is forfeit. The court also has the power to order compensation; where this order would fall upon the parents it must be established that they have not exercised full and proper care and control over their children. The parents, however, must be given the right to be heard.

The Act sees these provisions as the limits of the power of the courts; when the Act is fully in operation the court will no longer have the right to order directly any form of custodial treatment, for part of the provision of the Act allows for the removal from the court of the power to order detention or to make an Attendance Centre Order.

The main effect of these provisions is to make all decisions concerning the child's removal from home the responsibility of the social worker, or the probation officer in collaboration with the social worker; when it is a question concerning the children under fourteen the decision is likely to be that of the social worker. The role of the probation service in the juvenile courts is a diminishing one.

The magistrates will no longer be involved in detailed decisions as to the kind of treatment a child or young person will receive; the social worker, within the limits of the particular order, will make the decisions.

This, surely, is right; the social worker has the fullest background information available and will know in much more detail and at closer hand the particular conditions of the child or young person. His attention will not be distracted from the offender by the offence.

His concern will be the long-term future of the child within the community and he will make his decisions and disposition in the light of that concern.

Supervision orders can be made for up to three years, but no longer; care orders may remain in force until the child or young person reaches the age of eighteen.

Power to revoke the order exists, and an application can be made to the court either by the social worker or by the parents and child or young person.

The social worker must exercise judgement over placing the child, and even if, as a result of a care order, a child is removed from home for any time during the period of the order, the child can be restored to his home at any time, if, in the judgement of the social worker, this is beneficial.

In criminal proceedings the court has the same powers as mentioned above, but with certain additions. The court can also give an absolute or conditional discharge, as previously; it is free to fine the offender up to a limit of £50 and can order payment of damages or compensation. It can also, at the moment, order detention or attendance at a centre, although this provision, as indicated earlier, is expected to disappear when the intermediate treatment, a new concept, is brought in.

Few intermediate treatment orders have been introduced so far, and the schemes are not yet working fully. This subject will be dealt with in much greater detail in Chapter 10; suffice it to say, at this stage, that intermediate treatment is, as its name implies, a supervision order with attached conditions, which is intermediate between an order which suggests treatment in the community and an order which suggests the possibility of treatment removed from the community.

It is a new device, attempting to hold the child or young person in the community and to provide further treatment, at the suggestion of the social services department, but backed by an order of the court, in an effort to help the child or young person in trouble.

Another part of the Act—not yet fully operative—changes the range of facilities available to the court and social workers. Before the 1969 Act there were local authority children's homes, reception centres, and some institutions and homes run by voluntary bodies which regularly received children into care, along with approved schools and remand homes which took children on order from the court. The Act set up Regional Planning

Committees, drawing their personnel from various groupings of neighbouring authorities, whose aim was to reconsider existing facilities for care, observation and assessment.

Twelve such Regional Planning Committees have been established and have been working since the first parts of the Act were brought into operation. They will devise a system of community homes for the future. This provision must respond to the needs of future generations of children, as the working of the Act reveals them. These committees are also concerned with intermediate treatment, and are charged with devising ways of making that part of the Act workable.

Obviously they must look at the resources of their regions in terms of buildings and people. Their schemes are then submitted to the Department of Health and Social Security, where they are considered and approved. Much will depend on the work of these committees and further consideration will be given to their work later in this book.

This chapter has attempted to summarise the main provisions of the Act. Various sections of the Act call for much more detailed discussion and this will emerge in later chapters. Inevitably in summarising in this fashion there is the danger of giving a false picture or a wrong emphasis to certain of the provisions. Since, also, the Act is being introduced piecemeal, the view of the final implications of the Act must in some measure be speculative.

3

First Reactions to the 1969 Act

Probably the first time the 1969 Act caught the public's attention was as a result of the outcry raised by certain of the members of benches of juvenile courts throughout the country about the deficiencies of the Act.

> Magistrates in Britain's juvenile courts believe that children under the age of seventeen can now commit almost any kind of crime with impunity as a result of the controversial Children & Young Persons Act, 1969, which came into operation almost two years ago. They believe that the Act has made the law irrelevant and an object of mockery among young people. (*The Times*).

Various magistrates and benches protested in letters to the press, the Magistrates' Association (who opened a special file), the Home Office, the Secretary of State for the Department of Health and Social Security and many others, that they were no longer able to 'protect the long suffering public against the depredation of a class of persons who are now apparently beyond the law'.

These were startling assertions, especially to some other members of juvenile court panels. Despite the concern shown by one section of magistrates, they were in another article taken to task as a whole for not doing their duty.

The title was a question: WHOSE SIDE ARE THEY ON?, with a banneret inserted over, emblazoned, 'The first duty ... is the protection of society'. The article then took the magistrates to task for a manifest bias towards the accused, for a lack of knowledge or understanding of the problems with which they were dealing, for 'fussing over' offenders, and then exhorted them to 'conduct criminal proceedings fairly'. This suggested that all the clerks to juvenile courts in the country were in dereliction of duty along with the magistrates.

The article concluded with a general warning to the public in the following terms:

The war on crime will not be won if adolescent offenders are dealt with by justices who behave like a nursery governess puzzled by the unaccountable naughtiness of dear little Christopher Robin.

The quotations are taken from two of our major national daily newspapers, both of which pride themselves on their responsible attitude to current social questions and give a great deal of space to matters of social policy and public concern. More emotive language was used in some other newspapers.

Such reports left little doubt that a crisis point had been reached in administering the law concerning children and young people. The fact that it was only one more ripple in a continuing crisis was overlooked. What had happened? Some readers may also wonder if the Act referred to in these excerpts bears any relation to the Act summarised in the last chapter.

However, for anyone familiar with the history of legislation in this field, this was an expected phenomenon; the 1969 Act like all its predecessors, had drawn attention to a perennial problem; public consciousness about such matters only seems to operate in fits and starts. This new start had brought on a pronounced fit.

The Act raised many problems, and the magistrates as a body were well aware of them. So were most other people who worked in the courts or with the children who appeared in the courts. The problems were not unknown to those who introduced the Bill, and were not left unexplored in the passage of the Bill through both Houses of Parliament on its way to becoming an Act.

Throughout the 1960s there were demands that children in trouble should be removed from the court process altogether. The solution proposed was to place them in the care of the Children's Departments of local authorities, who since their establishment in 1948 had developed a body of skill and expertise in dealing with these problems.

It must not be overlooked, however, that not all children in trouble were dealt with by the Children's Departments, and there were other local authority departments and other agencies at work. This was one of the difficulties which had faced the Ingleby

Committee and its failure to deal boldly and decisively with the
tangle rendered part of the report less effective than it might have
been. In fact the 1969 Act was introduced in part to make good
that failure.

It was known to the Home Office, who were responsible for
introducing the Bill, that the local authorities were not properly
staffed nor equipped to deal with the total problem; indeed at
this stage, a great deal of argument took place about the timing
of the Act. Those who took the decision to go ahead knew that
they were introducing new legislation before the local authorities
were properly organised to undertake their new responsibilities.
But their view was that if the Act had to await ideal circumstances,
it would never become law. The Act would draw attention to
deficiences in the social machinery; the drive to make good the
deficiencies would then be that much more energetically pursued
on all levels. This is a legitimate point of view; very often any
advance is resisted in the name of perfection.

Moreover, whatever the defects of the Ingleby Committee
report, and the 1963 Act, the Children's Departments had been
given power, if they wished to use it, to devise programmes of
preventive work. Their response, except in a few instances, had
not been impressive. The Act was, therefore, in one sense,
intended to shock the local authorities into carrying out a task
for which they already had powers and had failed to undertake,
and to back that shock with pressure from the courts.

The difficulties, or at least some of them, were foreseen. It
happened that the difficulties were compounded by government
action in other directions.

Two other pieces of legislation came into effect which critically
affected the working of the Children and Young Persons Act.
The Local Authority Social Services Act, 1970, became operative
at about the same time as the Children and Young Persons Act.
Under this Act the children's departments disappeared; new
social services departments were set up, where children in trouble
were only part of the responsibility of a much more widely
based service, dealing with all those in need in our society, the
old, the handicapped, the sick and the inadequate.

At the same time the reorganisation of local government was
in train. New authorities were being set up with new boundaries
and differing powers; there were inevitably changes of staff and
new sets of officers were brought together. This meant that the

Children and Young Persons Act was only a minor surge in a process of upheaval; the miracle is that any service at all was maintained during that initial period.

It is always distressing to be involved in such a turmoil; the greatest care was taken to see that those most directly concerned, the children and young people, were least affected. Nevertheless, on all sides, and at all levels, there was disturbance. It also meant, more interestingly, that the whole situation was extremely fluid, and it may mean, at the end of the day, when the confusion is less, that a new and more responsive pattern will emerge. There are some signs that this is a possibility, but we are not yet far enough away from the area of upheaval to make any firm judgement. Nor must it be overlooked that in the course of the upheaval there may have been damage and suffering to those children who were the concern of the social service departments at that time.

There have been other effects; the Act has precipitated crises of role, confidence and practice amongst many of the social workers who were caught up in the transformation; many defects in the system of care and concern have been revealed. These have not necessarily been caused by the Act; they were there and observable before the Act came into being. Smoother working relationships and well established routines may have served to cover over many defects which the upheavals of the past few years have brought under fresh scrutiny. In the end it may all be for the good.

There is one other factor which must be taken into account. Between the passing of the Act and the implementation of its first stage there was a change of government. It is doubtful whether the 1969 Act, even if some such measure had been contemplated by the ministers who became responsible for its administration, would have been in the form that they inherited, or whether it would have commanded the same priority in the minds of those ministers. Certainly there has not been evidenced the necessary drive to make good, in terms of resources and policies, the shortcomings of the services which are supposed to make the Act a reality, though it is not fair to imply that this is a result of the change. Indeed, the subsequent change of government has revealed no greater sense of urgency so far.

As a result of the reorganisation of the social services at both local and national level, the Home Office, which for years had, through its Children's Department, borne responsibility for much of the work, lost its functions and its personnel to the Department of Health and Social Security. At one period, in response to outcry and pressure, both the Home Secretary and the Secretary of State were issuing joint statements, which highlighted the upheaval and the transitional state in which affairs were at the time.

However, it is a transitional phase only; the lines of communication are much clearer once more, and the patterns of responsibility are becoming properly defined. What is certain is that the social services departments, strive as they might, are not yet organised to carry through in full the duties now laid upon them by the Act. It is also certain that the local authorities have not been given the necessary financial support from national government to prepare themselves properly to undertake these new responsibilities. This is a matter which will have to be looked at again, but when any outcry is raised it is important to look beyond the local courts and the local authorities to central government. The solutions are not so simple as those who raised the initial outcry would have the public believe.

The minority of magistrates who protested vehemently did neither the magistracy nor anyone else much service. It is not reassuring to the public to see such an intemperate reaction from those who are expected to exercise judgement impartially and arrive at sound conclusions in an atmosphere of calm. Even given that there was a crisis, their protest was ill-directed. When the first noise and fury subsided, the impression left in the minds of the general public (apart from a possible general unease) was that the magistrates were angry because they had lost the right to make Approved School orders.

The magistrates (or those who made the most noise) were showing a touching faith in the approved schools, which was hardly justified by their past record. The real problems were lost sight of in the hysteria of the first outburst; most of those are still with us.

The direction of many attacks was against the social workers and the social services departments of the local authorities. The idea that a 'young social worker' (they were always young!) could know better than an experienced bench was not an acceptable proposition. This gave rise to what has been called the 'mini-skirted dolly-bird' syndrome! It always seemed to be the judgement of a 'mini-skirted, dolly-bird' female social worker that the magistrates took greatest exception to.

There were few such to be seen in the courts that I sat in; for the most part they were welcome if for no other reason than that they were good to look at. It is always a mistake to confuse sartorial matters with competence; a few of my colleagues might be prone to such an error, but they are not many. It interested me that, when fashion changed, a new epithet emerged: 'the betrousered baggage!'. Significantly the sex did not change. I have quoted both epithets carefully because often the choice of word and phrase is far more revealing than those who use them appreciate.

It would all be trivial in the extreme, were it not an indication of real problems of concern which emerge only under conditions of stress. What the Act did was to call into question the role of the magistrates and the social workers; that is something which is of importance.

How the Juvenile Court Works

The juvenile court magistrate has always had a difficult role, which derives in part from the nature of the court itself.

Originally established as a court of summary jurisdiction, it carries with it all the judicial functions of such a court; nevertheless, it has always had to pay attention to the fact that those who came into it as defendants had been set apart for particular consideration and special treatment by reason of their age.

Lawyers always approach the court strictly as a court of law and insist on the pre-eminence of that function; others who have to turn to the court will press other considerations upon it.

The court has two functions: one as a tribunal of proof, the other as an assessor of provision for treatment of those in trouble who come to its notice. In a sense the dividing line between the two functions falls between trial and sentence, although in this context 'disposal' is possibly a more suitable word. The court has to contain these two functions within one structure; similarly, those people who make up the court must possess the skills and qualities required for both these different functions.

One thing remains clear: where an allegation of an offence is made, that offence must be stated clearly and in comprehensibly specific terms and be proved to the full satisfaction of the court, by tests which are as strict as those in any other court. While the courts remain, this will always apply, and rightly so.

The rules of evidence, the burden of proof on the prosecution, the rights of the defence, the conduct of the court must not depart from the strictest standards applied in every other court; if they do so, then there is always a higher court to reverse wrong process and issue the necessary strictures. The juvenile court is under the same scrutiny as every other court in the land and it must be conducted in a way which will satisfy that scrutiny on all counts and on all occasions.

Some police officers, some social workers and various other people who come into court, are, at times, likely to misunderstand the position. Because the procedure is made as informal as possible, they come to believe that there is some relaxation in the application of the normal legal standards. This is not so, and the court should be zealous in maintaining the proper standards and ensuring that all others live up to them as well. Even some less experienced advocates, when they first come into a juvenile court, seem prone to take the same view; they also need to be reminded that it is a false one.

It is particularly dangerous when magistrates also succumb to this way of thinking; and every member of the bench should guard against it at all times.

The court has basically two types of case to hear: Care proceedings under Section I of the Act and Criminal proceedings under Section II of the Act. In criminal matters the procedure and requirements are more clearcut: an offence is alleged and that offence has to be proved to the standards outlined earlier.

The bench has two functions even during the hearing of criminal proceedings, and these need to be distinguished; it acts in part as judge, in part as jury.

As judge, under the guidance of the clerk of the court, the bench is responsible for the proper conduct of the hearing; when all the evidence is in, the bench must then decide if there is a case to answer, and if it decides there is, then it will proceed to hear the defence. When both prosecution and defence evidence is in, and the bench has listened to any representations in respect of the law, and any address that defence counsel wish to make to it, it retires, and then it assumes its role as a jury.

Criminal proceedings, under the Act, will apply only to young persons, that is, those over the age of fourteen. For those under the age of fourteen, Section I of the Act applies; these children will be brought before the court on a summons under Section I, for care proceedings.

Care proceedings are more like civil action; and in making a decision a less exacting standard of proof is required, except in the case where an alleged offence has been committed. When this is so, it has to be proved to the same standard and in precisely the same way as in criminal proceedings against an older young person; in other words the required standard of proof is 'beyond reasonable doubt'.

For any other form of care proceedings, the standard of proof is lower, less exacting and less well defined; it is normally reached 'on the balance of probabilities'. It is, however, no less challenging to the bench.

In care proceedings a 'double proof' is, in fact, needed. The court must first of all be satisfied that the child is being neglected or exposed to moral danger or is beyond control or is truanting; these conditions will be established on the basis of 'balance of probabilities'. Or the court must be satisfied that the child has committed an offence; this must be established on the basis of proof 'beyond reasonable doubt'—this is such an important point that I offer no apology for making it more than once.

If, and when, the first part has been established, the court must turn to a further matter: whether or not it has been proved that there is an overriding need of 'care or control which the child is unlikely to receive unless the court makes an order'.

The level of proof required for this second set of facts is also on a 'balance of probabilities'. And this second test has to be applied to a child under fourteen who has had an offence proved against him. The fact that an offence has been proved against the child is not enough in itself to entitle the court to proceed to making an order.

Some courts, unfortunately, do not seem to be so scrupulous in this matter as the Act enjoins; I have sat as an observer in courts and seen the bench move from giving an opinion on the offence to the consideration of disposal of the case without pausing to apply the second part of the test at all; every time this is done it is wrong.

It can be seen from this simplistic outline of some of the duties falling to the bench that the roles it is called upon to play in the hearing and disposal of a single case are many, varied and complex. Every member of the bench must have a clear understanding of the type of process, the different stages in the development of the process, and a thorough knowledge of their duties and functions at each of these stages.

CRIMINAL PROCEEDINGS

This initial truncated account of the two forms of process does not touch upon many of the finer shades of interpretation of the law and is, in a sense, a travesty of a description; I have set it out in this fashion to try to leave certain outlines as stark as possible, so that they may also be as clear as possible. It in no way represents even a small part of the function of the bench, even though it does touch upon the central core of the bench's duty, which is to administer the law within the provisions of the Act.

There are, however, many other factors to which the bench must pay heed. The whole 'tone' of the court is set by the bench; if the court is to work properly it has to pay particular and careful attention to this more amorphous factor as well, at every sitting.

It is important to explain what is meant by 'tone' in this context. It takes in the whole ambience of the court, the way people are brought to court, the way they are received when they arrive, how they are introduced into the court, how they are addressed at all times, in the waiting-rooms outside the court and in the court itself. These are vital considerations in ensuring that justice is done, that it is seen to be done, and that it is felt to be done.

A youngster is summoned to appear in court; he arrives at the time stated on the summons. The first person he will speak to, probably, will be the usher. The usher's manner, tone of voice, courtesy or lack of it, patience in explaining matters, and general demeanour are all significant in the way the court is run; they are especially important to those who are strange to courts and are under stress because of the ordeal they are about to face.

The child will have some time to spend in the waiting-room, unless he is extremely fortunate; the waiting-room should be as comfortable and convenient as possible. The time will arrive when he will be called into court. He should be found and brought in, again by the usher, with the courtesy due from one citizen to another, for that is what they all are.

That fact applies also within the court room itself. The bench, the clerk to the court, all other officers of the court, and everyone in the court are all fellow citizens, gathered, as it happens, within a court of law and therefore working within certain rules that the law enjoins, to enquire into an allegation concerning those who have been summoned. The common decencies, as between fellow citizens, apply at all times in the court room, despite its formalities and because of its stresses.

The chairman of the bench, as spokesman for the bench as a whole, has a first duty to ensure that those before the court understand their rights fully. On first appearance, for instance, he should explain as clearly, briefly and simply as possible why the summons has been issued, and the rights of the child or young person to legal aid. This should be done even before a plea is taken, because a different sort of plea might be entered if legal advice were at hand.

Of course, if the defendant is already represented, these matters will be looked after by his representative; if there is no representation, and the defendant and parents do not wish for, or will not accept, legal representation, then the plea may be taken.

It is usually the task of the clerk of the court to put the charge; this is done in as clear, straightforward and jargonless a form as possible, such as:

'Tom, they say you took such-and-such from a (specified place) when you knew you had no right to it and that it was not yours.'

There will be a response to this; if it is a denial then the plea is not guilty. For a child under fourteen there will be a further question: 'Did you know it was wrong to do (whatever is alleged)?' If the child says no, then a short dialogue must ensue, to establish if the claim is justified or not. If the court decides that the child really did not know that it was wrong, taking into account his age and understanding, then the case is at an end.

Where the case continues and the allegation is denied, then the chairman, as spokesman of the bench, must explain the procedure which has to be followed. It is important to do this for many reasons: not least to enable the unrepresented to take proper advantage of every right the law allows them.

My own feeling is that children should always be represented; even those cases which at first sight seem simple and straightforward can raise quite complex and subtle points of law, which can only be dealt with properly by a legal mind working on behalf of the defendant. Very often it falls to the bench to try to persuade the defendant and parents of the need for legal representation; very often their own view is simplistic—'He did it, or you say he did it. Let's get on with it and get it over with!'

On occasion, even where the bench succeeds in impressing upon parents and child the need to be legally represented, and then explains that the case will have to be adjourned in order to allow time for the preparation of the defence, there will be grumblings, and sometimes an attempt to change the plea again.

In a busy court, working under pressure, with a large number of cases on its list it is easy for this to happen, because it is understandable, very human and convenient. (It may also be the private view of the bench that there is not much of a defence to be made, anyway: this is an improper conclusion to draw and a wrong basis for making a decision, and yet I have heard things implying just such an attitude spoken all too frequently.)

The bench should not allow such a change of mind or plea without the most scrupulous enquiry; it must ensure that the change of mind is genuine, and that no undue pressure is being applied on the parents by any other person, nor on the defendant by the parents; it is the child or young person who must answer the allegation, and the court must ensure that it is the child or young person's plea which is heard.

There are other occasions when the defendant admits the allegation, and then, later, when giving some account of what happened, reveals circumstances which indicate that the admission was wrong. The bench should immediately order that the admission be struck out and arrange that the case be heard by another bench. Again there may be protests from the parents or the defendant about the waste of time (a fair observation), but the bench should persist and not acquiesce in a possible wrong plea because of inconvenience either to themselves or anyone else.

They should always be on the alert for other pressures either on the defendant or on them. There are over-eager policemen, who may feel that there is no defence or, who, eager for a conviction, may have advised the defendant or the defendant's parents outside the court, who themselves do not wish to come back to court again.

These decisions are the sole responsibility of the bench, under advice from the clerk of the court. The bench must take very great care at the outset to ensure that all these matters are fully explained, and that his rights as the defendant are put to the child and his parents.

I made reference earlier to an apparently simple case which can have complex and subtle interpretations. Take, for example, the theft of a bicycle. A child may have seen a bicycle outside a shop, got on it, ridden away and been stopped. It happens every day. The child, if the matter is put to him in court, will say, 'Yes, I did it.'

The law, quite properly, cannot allow things to remain there, even though these may be the facts. There is the matter of intent: Did the child intend to deprive the owner of the bicycle permanently? Or was he intending to ride it around a little and then take it back roughly to where he took it from? If the latter, it cannot be theft. If, of course, he has kept the bike for several days, and concealed it meanwhile, and ridden it occasionally, the claim that he intended to restore it to the owner loses a great deal of force.

These are matters that, in the best circumstances, would be explained to the child by a legal representative; failing that, the court has to attempt to draw it from the defendant. It is often bewildering for youngsters and parents to have certain questions of this sort put to them, yet it is necessary. At all times the court should explain with as much lucidity and simplicity as possible what the issues are, without improperly suggesting a defence which is false, and what the process in court is about. I have tried to recall approximately what I say in such circumstances.

Listen very carefully to what I am about to say. The court is going to be told what *they* say you did. In other words they are going to tell us their side of the story. Each person who knows something about what happened will come and tell us what they saw or heard. You must listen closely to each one. When they have told us what they know, you have the right to ask them questions about what they have said. You can do this for each one in turn, directly they have finished. If there is anything they say you disagree with or which you do not think is fair, you must ask a question about it. If you cannot think of a question, but there is something you disagree with, then you must tell us, and we will try to help you to put a question on that point.

When we have heard what they say, your turn comes. You will then have the chance to tell us your side of the story. Do you understand all that, so far? ... It is in two parts. Their side, first—you asking any questions. Then, your side—and they can ask you questions. You can always ask your parents to help you.

We will listen to what is said, and to the questions and answers, and then it is our job, at the end of it all, to make up our minds about what we've heard and say if it has been proved or not.

It is long; in the course of a day and a number of repetitions, it can become very tedious. Nevertheless, either this or something similar must be said. It may, on occasion, be the sixth, seventh or even tenth time I have had to say it in the court and everyone else in the court has heard me recite it—except for the defendant and his or her parents, and that is the important point: for them it is the only time.

We can then proceed to the case. It may be necessary, as I have indicated, to help the unrepresented child and parents to devise or frame questions in cross-examination. It may also be necessary to explain the difference between asking questions and trying to make assertions of innocence or accusing witnesses of lying. These are matters about which the bench must be continually on the alert and continually patient. At the same time, always with the help and guidance of the clerk of the court, it is important to see that only proper evidence is introduced from either side, and that nothing improper is brought into the case.

The chief difficulty regarding evidence is the matter of hearsay. It is sometimes difficult, even with experienced witnesses, to make them understand that what someone told them happened is not evidence. Despite the complexities, the best guide for the lay magistrate is the test of what is best evidence; best evidence is what the witness saw or heard directly. It is dangerous to allow any witness to draw any inference or conclusion from what they saw; these must be made by the bench at the proper time.

After the prosecution has made its case comes the first pause for consideration. The bench must decide whether the prosecution has made a sufficiently good case for them to require the defendant to answer it.

The test in the mind of the bench at this moment is not whether the case has been proved 'beyond a reasonable doubt', but rather that there is, on the basis of what has been said so far, reason for the defendant to account for where he was, what he was doing and why he was doing it at the time stated. In many instances this is not a difficult decision to make; when it is, the court should rise and the bench retire to consider the matter in full.

If they decide that there is no case to answer, then they should return to court and dismiss the case. They should not ever, at this stage, reason on the following lines: 'Well, there might be something in it. Let's see what the defendant says!' They are then looking to the defendant to convict himself. If they feel that there is not a proper and sufficient case to answer, that should be the end of the matter.

In such circumstances they should then turn to the routine consideration of the award of costs. It does not mean that the bench feels that the prosecution has acted wrongly or improperly in bringing the case (although many policemen tend to react as if this were so); a case may have seemed to have had substance on the basis of statements given by witnesses, who failed, in court, to live up to the tests the court requires. But if a case has lacked substance to such a degree that it is dismissed without the defence being called, then the defendant has been placed in jeopardy and under stress, and the parents put to considerable inconvenience and expense. The least the court can do is to consider reimbursement of the losses which the appearance has occasioned: fares, loss of earnings and any other proper expense.

In my experience too few benches consider this matter at the right time; very often the unrepresented defendant and the parents are so relieved that they do not think to ask for costs. It is up to the bench to make such award as they think fit. It is only just to do so. In cases where the child is represented, it is up to the representative to make the application. The bench should never flinch from its duty in this matter because it thinks an award might reflect adversely on the career of any officer of the court—that is not a matter which can properly concern them at all.

In the case of an unrepresented defendant, once the court decides that what it has heard from the prosecution has, on the face of it, established a case to answer, then it will say so; the bench must now turn to the defence. It is necessary to explain to the defendant: 'It is now your turn to tell us your side of the story.' Even this is not so simple: there are various decisions the defendant must make, in consultation with his parents.

You can say nothing, if you wish. If you say nothing, I must warn you that the court will have to make up its mind on what it has heard so far, without hearing your side of the story. Do you want to tell us your side of the story?

If the answer is no, there is no way, nor should there be, of compelling the defendant to give his evidence. Usually a youngster is only waiting his chance to put his side of the case. When he indicates this, there is still one more decision for him to make.

If you want to tell us your side of the story, there are two ways in which you can do it. You can go over there, make a promise to tell the truth, as all the others have done so far, and tell us about it all from there. If you choose to do that, you can be asked questions in turn, to test what you say.

Very often the youngster starts off to take his place in the witness stand; but there is something more which has to be said.

There is one other way. You may remain where you are. You can tell us what you want to say, or what you think is important, without promising to tell the truth. I must warn you that then we cannot help you in any way, by telling you where or how to begin, or telling you when to stop. It is all up to you.

I think I should also say that, on the whole, we are more likely to believe someone who makes a promise to tell the truth and who is willing to answer questions about what they say. But the decision is yours, what do you want to do?

Again the process is rather long and can seem tedious, but has to be done, in something like this form, for each and every defendant. No pressure should be brought upon the defendant to make a quick decision and full opportunity should be given for the child or youth to consult with his parents.

Usually, as I have said, the defendant is bursting to go into the witness stand to tell the other side of the case. In those cases where they do not wish to do so, and remain where they are, without promising to tell the truth (making, technically, an unsworn statement), there is very real difficulty. It may be that a long and rambling account is given to the court, which is not pertinent to the facts at all, and does not bring out matters which might be of importance. The bench can help in no way, neither by indicating where to begin, nor what matters to bring out nor where to end. That is the law, and it is not very satisfactory, and all the careful explanation beforehand on the part of the bench may be of no use. Indeed, in these circumstances, the defendant may say things which do real harm to his case. It is at this time in particular that I feel very strongly that a child should be represented in court, because no defendant so young should be put in such an unhelpful position.

If, on the other hand, the defendant chooses to give evidence, having made a promise to tell the truth, the clerk can do something to evince the facts: first he establishes the identity of the defendant, then he continues with carefully chosen and modulated questions of a neutral character, to help the defendant tell his story and put the facts in issue before the court. Even this is not the most satisfactory process, but all courts see it happen every day, and will continue to do so until all children are represented in court.

The bench should remain as alert as before. They must be particularly careful to see that the defendant does not introduce irrelevant matters which may harm his case. A child, protesting his innocence, may suddenly make reference to his supervising officer or to some other occasion when he was in trouble with the police or other agency—an inference which may damage him in the eyes of the bench. It is not always possible to prevent this happening; the bench must rigorously exclude such matters from its mind when considering its final verdict.

Very often there are difficulties, particularly with unrepresented defendants, about 'best' evidence and 'hearsay'. On each occasion the bench must explain with great care and courtesy why something cannot be said, or why it cannot be said in that fashion; or indicate that perhaps someone else, a parent, friend, brother, sister or bystander can say it, when the defendant cannot. Every effort should be made by the court to enable the defendant to make his defence fully. A peremptory interruption, without explanation, may serve to silence the witness and prevent him from saying something which might be relevant and important. This applies to all the witnesses that the defendant calls. His right to call witnesses must be explained to him, and if need be the court must be willing to adjourn the case to hear the witnesses, should they not be available at the time; the court must also be prepared to give any help required in bringing them there.

Finally, the last evidence will be heard. When the defendant is represented, the representative will possibly call witnesses as to character, and address the bench on the law and the facts. A similar opportunity must be given to the unrepresented defendant, but again there are great difficulties, as can readily be appreciated. The unrepresented defendant is once more at a manifest disadvantage. When there is no one else to plea for him, it must be done by the bench, if only mentally, when they come to retire.

At last, the bench will retire. Its deliberations are its own. The lay bench, consisting usually of three people, really decides the issue on the basis of a jury discussion. The chairman, in such a discussion, is likely to be the most experienced member of the bench, but his views carry no more weight than the least experienced member of the bench. There is no form of casting vote. It has always been my own practice as a chairman, on retirement, not to indicate my own point of view initially. It is important to study the specific allegation once more, to refresh the minds of all the members of the bench, see what is required to be proved, be quite clear on the law of the case, and itemise the matters which are contentious between the prosecution and the defence.

Having done this, we can discuss such points as arise. When we have completed this process I usually call upon my two colleagues to tell me what they think, calling upon the less experienced first, and passing, without comment, to the second of my colleagues. If they agree, there is no need for me to express an opinion at all. The decision is taken on a majority, and if they are firm in their opinions, then the matter is decided.

It might be that any one of us might be in violent disagreement with the other two. This seldom happens in practice, and is not a happy situation; when it does, the dissent must be resolved if possible by careful discussion. Even if a majority decision is arrived at in this way, with one member of the bench in total disagreement with the other two, the decision remains the decision of the whole bench. I make no apology for repeating that the decision must be made on the basis of 'beyond reasonable doubt'; the burden of proof is placed upon the prosecution—it is not the task of the defence to establish innocence, only to raise sufficient doubt.

This account, then, has brought the process in criminal proceedings to the establishment of proof. It is useful to leave the matter there for a moment and turn to the other form of process: care proceedings.

CARE PROCEEDINGS
In criminal proceedings the prosecution is most likely to be brought by the police; in care proceedings it is most likely that the local authority will make the allegation.

This allegation has to be put clearly. There is a real difficulty in that often the proceedings are brought because the child is being neglected or treated in some way which has caused him harm or is likely to cause harm in the future. The allegation is often therefore partly directed against those responsible for the child's upbringing, rather than against the child. In other words, there is no single defendant.

In those cases where truancy is alleged, the local education authority will make the allegation, by introducing school attendance figures. These must be put to the child and parents, and they must agree that they are true and then be asked to account for the non-attendance; the court should be told of any illness, and doctor's certificates can be introduced to back up these claims; any other factors which the court should know of should also be given.

In cases of neglect there will be other evidence from the Social Services Department, from the police, or from an officer of the National Society for the Prevention of Cruelty to Children; very often there will be photographs, which have to be properly introduced. Often there will be evidence of a finding of guilt against the parents from a hearing in another court.

For other cases of neglect or moral danger, evidence as to the conduct of the child or young person will be given: the company he or she keeps, what hours they keep, the places they frequent, the time they come in at night, if they have slept rough or run away from home. Usually this is given by a social worker. At each stage all such evidence is subject to challenge by either the child or the parents.

These cases, even though 'civil' in nature, now carry by statute the same right to free legal aid as criminal cases; again it is important that this should be explained both to the child and the parents. It may be necessary for the child to be offered legal aid independent of any arrangements that the parents may wish to make; this is a point the court should be particularly careful about.

Very often these proceedings are more difficult to preside over than criminal cases. The allegation is more diffuse; the points at issue can be less precise; there can be a feeling that the allegation is only being made for 'the good of the child'. This may, in fact, be true, but it does not discharge the bench from any part of its duties in the matter.

Very often, also, the social workers who will be giving evidence and possibly conducting the case are not very familiar with the role; for a number of them it is a task which is undertaken with a certain reluctance, not to say, on the part of some, repugnance. Their understanding of what is, and what is not, evidence, is not so precise; there is also a danger that they will make assertions which they feel are valid, which turn out to be incapable of proof, and so are not evidence. Most courts are still feeling their way to the best form of procedure in hearing these cases; the difficulty arises because they are less 'cut and dried' than criminal hearings, by which I mean that there is no longer such a clear distinction between the parties, as there is in the 'gladiatorial contest' of prosecution and defence in criminal proceedings.

Benevolence of intent cannot make good a bad case. But the social worker is in real difficulty. Much of his evidence is obtained from conversations with the parents and defendant in the course of attempting to help them in a difficult situation; suddenly the child and parents find these matters introduced into a court process and used (in their view) against them.

Moreover much of the evidence is concerned with social work; it takes account of factors other than the law allows; it has considerations from another profession informing it—and sometimes, in the making of a case, these considerations are imported. Because the lines are less well drawn, and because of the stress in such a situation on both the social workers and the parents and children, tensions can arise which are absent from criminal proceedings and are less easily guarded against. The role of the police officer in criminal proceedings is understood, if not always appreciated, by the child and parents; very often the social worker is looked upon as a betrayer, and in the resultant bitterness, matters which could be introduced on behalf of the child or parents are lost sight of or never properly brought out. The court, also, because it can be lulled into the attitude that the local authority is working in the best long-term interests of the child, can on occasion be rather less than vigilant.

It is not always clear to the parents that the local authority has had to consider very carefully the whole situation before bringing the case to court at all. Yet that is their duty. They should only bring the case when they are satisfied that conditions in the life of the child are such that an order made by the court is necessary, and that only such an order can safeguard the child.

The court will know this, but it still has to exercise its powers of scrutiny on behalf of the child; it must never become an ally of the social worker or the social services department and enter into a form of collusion to make an order, unless the allegation is proved and the case made good. If it were to do so, it would be doing wrong.

With all these difficulties the case should proceed in much the same way as was outlined earlier for criminal proceedings, so far as giving and testing evidence are concerned. At all times the same care should be taken to explain their rights to unrepresented children and parents.

At the end a decision will be taken on the facts; in care proceedings this is decided on the 'balance of probabilities'. But it must be remembered that the court's work is not done. The first decision will only have determined that the court is satisfied that the child's development, health or future is at risk. It must then consider separately whether the child 'is in need of care or control which he is unlikely to receive unless the court makes an order'. This is a separate decision and must be decided separately, and there may well be further representation needed from the local authority and from the child and parents before a decision is reached; an opportunity must be given to both parties, and their rights explained.

5

The Welfare of the Child

In both 'criminal' and 'care' proceedings this account of the working of the Act in court has now reached the same stage : the court has given a decision and has pronounced itself satisfied that some action is called for.

It is, in a sense, at this stage that the bench changes hats. Consideration of the welfare of the child or young person now comes fully into play.

The first duty of the court is to call for all possible, relevant information before making up its mind about the disposal of the case. The only occasion when the court would not call for such reports would be where it felt that the case was so trivial that reports were not necessary.

Under the new Act these reports will mostly be prepared and presented by the Social Services Department of the local authority. There are still powers to call upon the Probation Service to make reports where this seems more appropriate, but increasingly the common practice in most juvenile courts is to turn to the Social Services Department.

The wording in the Act is as follows:

Where a local authority or a local education authority brings proceedings under section I of this act or proceedings for an offence alleged to have been committed by a young person or are notified that any such proceedings are being brought, it shall be the duty of the authority, unless they are of the opinion that it is unnecessary to do so, to make such investigation and provide the court before which the proceedings are heard with such information relating to the home surroundings, school record, health and character of the person in respect of whom the proceedings are brought as appear to the authority likely to assist the court. (Section 9:1 *C.Y.P.A.* 1969.)

In cases where reports are not immediately available, or the court does not feel that they are sufficient for it to make up its mind, the court should adjourn the case so that all the required reports are available to it. The court may, for instance, need a psychiatric report; it is the duty of the local authority to ensure that all such specialist reports are made available, as well as those from its own social workers, at the next hearing.

The main report the court sees will have been made by a trained social worker. This report is of the utmost importance in the work of the court. The bench is completely dependent upon the skill, insight, knowledge and professional judgement of the social worker, for the picture the magistrates will form of the child or young person, and his or her parents, home and way of life will be refracted through the eyes of the social worker.

Their disposal of the case will largely turn upon the report, and the future of the child lies very much with the reporting officer—demanding much of his professional training and integrity. Much more will be said about the role of the social worker in the court and his wider role outside the court, where he is in contact with children, young people and their families, but even at this stage, the importance of the social worker and the report need all the emphasis that can be given.

There will always be a school report, unless the case concerns a young person who has been away from school for such a time that the court and social services feel it is no longer of much relevance; where the subject is of school age or has only recently left school (and under the new school-leaving age, this will include all the children and most of the young persons before the court), a school report must be available and studied.

What does a typical report look like? I have set out a concocted example on pp. 53–55. This has been compiled from my recollection of many hundreds of such reports, and is an attempt to include various pieces of information which occur in one form or another over a whole series of reports. This is the form of the report I would see in the juvenile court in South London where I usually sit; and while reports from other parts of the country may differ in layout and in some particulars, they will convey similar kinds of information and will be couched in much the same terms.

LONDON BOROUGH OF EXEHAM

Social worker: Miss E. Ford   *Court:* Camberwell Juvenile
Address: Area 5, 34 Holly Rd, S.E.27   *Date of hearing:* 23.1.74
Telephone: 774 12345 Ext. 6

SOCIAL WORKER'S REPORT
concerning

Full name: Thomas Richard Harry   *Born:* 8.11.60
Address: 123 Ivylawn Road, S.E. 27   *Age:* 14
                                 Religion: R.C.
School attended: St Francis Xavier, Whypool, Sussex (Community home)
(or occupation)

Matter before court: Burglary

Previous court appearances:
20.9.72   Camberwell Juvenile court:
    1. Theft of bundle of magazines
    2. Attempted theft from lorries
    3. Breaking gas meter
    Seven other offences taken into consideration.
    Care order to London Borough of Exeham.
1.12.73   Whypool Juvenile Court
    1. Breaking and entering
    2. Taking motor vehicle
    3. Driving under age
    4. Without insurance
    Fined £3 to be paid out of own pocket money.
    Conditional discharge on other offences.

FAMILY COMPOSITION
Father: Mr James Harry—tailor's finisher
Mother: Mrs Joyce Harry—two part-time jobs
Children: Thomas (subject)   8.11.60
           Wendy   23.12.63
           William   12.12.64

Accommodation
The Harry family are buying their own home, a small terraced house, on mortgage. Some rooms are as yet only sparsely furnished, but are being decorated and furnished as finance permits. A bathroom has recently been added. The home is clean and well kept, even though Mrs Harry has two jobs outside the home.

Employment
Mr Harry works full-time as a tailor's finisher, and his wife part-time as a school meals helper from Monday to Friday and at weekends as a domestic help in a hospital. This is necessary to meet the mortgage repayments. Their total weekly income is about £42.

Background
The family came to this country from Ireland about five years ago. Tom
is away from home during term-time but lives with his family during the
school holidays. His parents have worked very hard and long hours to try to
achieve security and good material standards for their children. Tom has
always caused the family some concern because of his 'mischief'. When his
parents first came to London Tom was left with his grandparents in Ireland.

Mr and Mrs Harry are aware of the strains that adaptation to life in
London have caused, but they have tried to help him and make allowances—
perhaps, at times, too many. Being the eldest child he seems to have felt
the change more than either of the other children. The parents now seem
bewildered and angered by Tom's behaviour; they feel very let down.

In the last few years he has run away from home about a dozen times.
He has caused considerable concern at school, and in the neighbourhood
by his behaviour; his parents have experienced some resentment on this
score.

When he ran away from home he tended to support himself by stealing
food from supermarkets and pilfering where he could. He truanted a great
deal from school, and took other children with him on occasions. Yet he
really has no friends.

At first it was thought that his stealing was merely in order to make
ends meet while he was truanting from school or running away from home.
The first offences of this nature were viewed in this light, and were not
brought to court. When finally he was brought to court a whole string of
offences were taken into consideration, and this authority asked for a
care order which was granted.

Tom was placed in St Francis School, a community home. The pattern
of his offences looks somewhat different now. The offences in the winter
of '73 involved him in stealing a car; he took two other boys from the school
with him on this expedition. They broke into a gas meter of a house close
to the school, took £5, came to London and spent the money in amusement
arcades, going to the pictures and on sweets and food. The three boys
were apprehended and returned to the St Francis School by the police.

At school the staff have been concerned by his lack of moral sense and
his lack of effort and progress. He plays football and shows a good sense
of sportsmanship on the field; he is also a good boxer. He has won trophies
for the school at both these sports.

Mr and Mrs Harry have tried various approaches to Tom. Beating him
did not work, so they have given this up. They now tend to try to bribe him
to be good by giving him frequent presents of money, clothing or whatever
else he asks for, within their limits. I have tried to explain to them that this
comes close to paying blackmail, and is not good either for him or them;
I think they have begun to realise this. The housemaster at school says that
if Tom wants something he has no idea of saving for it from his own pocket
money; he expects someone to provide it for him on demand. Some of the
demands he has made have been quite unreasonable; for example, a
motor-cycle, and, failing that, a chopper-bike.

Whilst at home he appears to relate fairly well to his siblings, but there
has been growing evidence of some bullying. His offences do not seem
to be triggered off by any unusual stresses or happenings within the family.
Tom himself says he does these things on the spur of the moment, and
expresses his regret at having committed these offences. One must wonder

whether the regret is at having done them or at having been caught. There does not seem to be much evidence of concern for the consequences of his actions either to himself or anyone else.

It is difficult to know how best to help this boy or suggest anything more than is being done already. It seems his present school is helping him about as much as any placement could be expected to do at the moment. His parents are anxious to help in any way they can, but they are really at the end of their resources, and are totally bewildered about what more they could do.

The care order is in operation and Tom is still at the St Francis School. I hope the court will see fit to take such action as will permit him to continue at the school, for the present, to see what progress is made over the next few months. I am sorry not to be more positive or helpful in the matter.

The report on pp. 53–55, as I must emphasise again, is a compilation. Its contents will, however, be familiar to most of those who work in the juvenile courts. It is a fair reflection of the sort of history which the court has to consider week in and week out. It is neither as dramatic as some nor as depressing as others.

After having received and read this report the bench must then talk to the subject and his parents about it. The law states specifically that the bench must tell the subject of the report, anything which bears upon his character or conduct and which may influence them in their decision. Parents must also be informed of any matter which gives information about their character, conduct or circumstances which may influence the bench.

In some courts, when the bench receive their copy of the report, the parents and child are given one as well. The Inner London courts have, for many years, adopted a different practice, which we trust adequately meets the requirements of the law, and yet, at the same time, ensures that the court is informed of all matters relevant to the case. The report is passed to the bench and before we begin to read it we tell the parents and child that this is the first time we have seen the report, that we will now proceed to read it, and then we will tell them what is in the report and discuss it with them before we make up our mind what we are going to do.

There are often matters which should properly be put before the bench which might be vital to the disposal of the case, but which could not be put in a report without causing great distress to the child or the parents.

For example, last year, I had a report which told me that the child, when younger, had been present in a house when a murder and suicide took place; it was not believed that the child had ever

fully understood just what had happened, but he had been in the
house some hours with two dead bodies before the tragedy was
discovered. This was important material in the history of the
child and something the bench should know.

But a court, with many strange and indifferent people in
attendance, would have been the last place for those facts to be
set so plainly before the child, for no matter how discreetly
framed, the damage resulting might have been incalculable. It
was something the court needed to know; it was not something
the child should be informed of for the first time, or reminded of
(whichever, in fact, might have applied—and no one could be
certain which did apply), at a time of great tension and stress.

On another occasion a report contained information that the
mother and father were not married: this meant that all the
children of their association were illegitimate; the children did
not know of this fact.

Many other matters occur from time to time which are just as
difficult and delicate. The likelihood of a divorce, a history of
violence in a marriage, the fact that one child of the family was
not the child of the father, the past criminal record of either
parent, the fact that either parent had been in prison or in a
mental hospital. Under the system we employ in London facts
can be presented unequivocably to the bench, but can be presented
differently to the parents and child.

The careful summary of a report calls for a degree of skill on
the part of the bench, but it is necessary if the court appearance
is not to do harm far beyond the immediate occasion of the
appearance. Again, let me give an example.

Not so long ago I had a report which dealt with the relationships
between the parents, and indicated that there had been considerable
difficulties at home, with the possibility of some violence between
husband and wife and the likelihood at one stage of a separation
or divorce. At a time when the court was wanting to keep the
child in the family, and yet needed to understand why he might
have been in the trouble which had brought him to court, it was
important for the court to have this information and yet do what
it could to reassure the child that the family still had a possible
future and a degree of stability.

The following dialogue might develop around this point.

'I understand, Mr and Mrs Brown, that there have been difficulties in your marriage.' Usually there will be a rather anxious

nod from mum and dad. 'It seemed, a few months ago, about the time of this trouble with Victor, that it was coming to a head.' Again, rather strained, defensive assent. 'Are things better now?' They indicate that they are.

I usually go on to say, 'I have fuller details than that in front of me. I want you to know that my colleagues and I have those details in the report and we must consider them. Do you want me to go into it in any more detail?'

Usually they will know, for their part, what the social worker has put in, and they will not be anxious to have the details rehearsed any further in court, especially in front of their child.

This system of working, and it can be much more subtle than this, remains within the spirit of the law; it enables the fullest and frankest reporting to the bench, and at the same time gives the parents the necessary leads to disagree if they feel that something is wrong or unfair. The same must be done in respect of the child. I would not leave the exploration of such a topic where I have broken off above; it would need further exploration, but I hope I have written enough to illustrate the technique adopted.

When the reports are in and have been considered and talked over, other further difficulties may arise. Supposing a child is in court for a fairly trivial offence, yet the report reveals that there are very serious problems in his life and home background. Where does the court direct its main concern and what weight does it give to the offence and to the offender?

There are various factors to take into account. It is, at this point, very often, that the dual role of the court, especially under the 1969 Act, raises particular difficulties and dilemmas.

The sense of fairness in the child ought not to be blighted, because this might lead to more serious trouble in the future: this is a very real possibility if the child feels that he has been dealt with harshly for a trivial offence, because of matters extraneous to the offence itself which emerge as a result of the social enquiries.

It is a nice and important point. In the end it has to be decided on the basis of the particular circumstances and by the common sense of the bench. One of the justifications for the continuance of the court system, in my view, is that, at this juncture, the bench is there to arbitrate between the child or young person and the social worker.

It may very well be that the child is in need of all sorts of help which can only be given through a court order. The local authority will have had to satisfy itself of that fact before allowing the matter to come to court in the first place, as it is enjoined to do by the Act. But the final decision is taken by the court; the court is there to apply just such a commonsensical point of view, the view of ordinary citizens, at this stage. It can be very difficult; the bench must not allow its own concern for the welfare of the child to intrude too far into its considerations, if that would undermine the concept of natural justice—because justice must be seen to be done, and felt to be done, by the child or young person.

The bench must not be swept along on the benevolent desire to do good or intervene which emanates from the social services department; it must examine the particulars of the case coolly and carefully. If, for something not too serious on the face of it, the bench does decide that an order must be made, which may seem harsh or unwarranted to the child or parents, it must explain the processes of its reasoning and the decision it has arrived at to both the child and parents, and attempt to win their co-operation in the course which it is proposing. Not to do so would create the possibility of considerable harm in the future, and might well destroy any possibility of co-operation between the family and the social worker, particularly if the family were to come to believe that it was because of the social worker that the court took a more serious view of the matter. It is even more difficult should there be more than one defendant.

For simplicity, let us take an example of two defendants, though sometimes there may be many more. Two boys come before the court; they have taken an equal part in a certain offence, something not too serious. They both admit to having done so. In due course the reports are produced. One of the children has a good home, concerned parents, who are shocked by what has happened, and who obviously will do all they can to ensure it will never happen again. There seems no reason in the child's background nor in their life together as a family to explain the involvement of the child in the offence. The other child comes from a different background; the parents do not care and seem to have little time for the child; it is not a good home and there are troubles between the parents, resulting in instability. The stresses of the family situation may well be affecting the child.

In the first case the social worker will probably report that the parents can cope. In the other they will indicate the need for some form of intervention through a court order. What is the court to do in such circumstances? What are the children's views?

If the court deals lightly with one child, and makes an order regarding the other, it will seem to the second child that he is having to suffer some form of control because of his parents' failure or some defect in his home, which may not be of his making or choosing. This is accentuated by the fact that the two children see themselves as equally involved and equally guilty.

There is also the damage done to the relationship between the child and parents; it may already be under some strain, and such a decision invites the child to reproach his parents, possibly coupled with resentment, and in their turn, his parents will feel guilt, failure and a sense of incapacity. Neither attitude is conducive to harmony within the family nor does it bode well for the child's future. To rely too heavily on a prediction of future trouble in the family might make the prophecy self-fulfilling. I have known of children, outraged by what they consider to be a wrong or harsh decision, leave the court and then proceed to commit a further offence, feeling in some way that they have earned the right to do so with impunity because they have been wrongly punished. I must draw attention to this point because the bench should bear it very much in mind when arriving at a decision and considering the reports.

Children have their own very discriminating sense of what is 'fair-play'; they seldom think in terms of 'justice', which is probably very wise. Their sense of 'fair-play' does not march with the law on all counts, but it is stupid to lose sight of it and insensitive to disregard it entirely.

It is easier to point to the dilemma than to suggest ways in which it can be resolved; generalising is dangerous. Each case will be different, and the circumstances of each case can never be matched with any other. If the court does decide to discriminate between two youngsters, it must make it clear that it knows it is doing so, and explain carefully what it hopes to achieve through such discrimination.

I have found it useful, on occasion, to put the whole issue before the child or young person concerned, and also to the parents, explaining that what the court is concerned about is not punishment (though you may never entirely succeed in convincing either the child or his parents of this but to discover the correct course to take to prevent the child getting into any more trouble in the future.

Very often the child and parents who have the dilemma put to them in this way will respond with surprising understanding and objectivity, and will see the sense of the proposed course of action. Even if the child or parents do not concur wholeheartedly, the discussion will at least have given them an insight into the processes of thought of the bench, and some understanding of why things turned out as they did. Better that, than allowing the child and parents to march out of court, smouldering with unvoiced resentment and confirmed in their mistrust of the court and the law; when that happens it is highly probable that the court will see both child and parents again.

This topic emphasises once again the importance of the 'tone' of the court, and the courtesy due to everyone in the courtroom. One further courtesy is that of a full explanation and discussion before a decision is announced. It is part of that respect which is due to everyone who comes into the court, whether witnesses, police officers, social workers, or in any other capacity, but especially the defendant and the defendant's parents.

This consideration can be taken a stage further; the effectiveness of the court depends in large measure on the degree of involvement of the child and parents which can be achieved. It may seem stupid to some people to make this point, since the whole proceeding is concerned with the defendant and through him with the parents. Nevertheless, very often, such is the state of tension and stress in the defendant and parents, that they may not be completely 'with' the court. The picture of the insolent, unconcerned, sometimes defiant young man or woman is a false one most of the time. What to the inexperienced eye might appear as unconcern, defiance, or any attitude of 'dumb insolence' is much more likely to arise through trying to put a brave face on a distressing situation than through bravado.

It is this need for involvement which has led me to place such stress on the careful explanation, at all stages, of what is going on; it is not only a requirement of the law, it is also vital to any future treatment which the court might recommend.

Part of this demands a degree of 'openness' on the part of the bench. It must always, as the law requires, explain the rights of the defendant and see that these are properly safeguarded; it must always make sure that the defendant understands what the various stages of the court process are about; it must also, at all times, make sure that what is happening and what is being said is comprehensible. If care is not taken it is very easy to allow the whole process to pass completely over the heads of the defendants and parents. They will only too readily assume that what they think, what they say, what they allege is not listened to as closely as what is said and alleged against them. If they ever form such an opinion and withdraw into themselves and from the process, then the court has demonstrably failed.

The court process should always be a dialogue; it cannot be, if one party, possibly the most affected, either cannot enter into it or chooses to assume that their contribution is not of importance or will not receive proper attention. They can then leave the court, escaping from an unpleasant experience, feeling that nothing that went on in the court was really their concern: that everything that happened, except perhaps the final punishment, had no reality for them. If they do quit the court in that mood, there is no real hope of success for any procedure of help or treatment that the court has ordered. The court will have served to confirm something that they may have chosen to suspect: that the law exists for other people, but not for them. This is the worst possible outcome, and is very sad.

Guarding against this is a long continuing battle, which has to be carried on through every case. Courtesy, concern and careful explanation at all stages are essentials; no court should ever be worried by wild accusations like those I quoted earlier, that it 'fussed' over the defendants, if all that is meant is that it took care to explain in the fashion I am advocating. However, that the court had behaved discourteously to anyone should be a cause for concern.

Those who work in the court regularly, the magistrates, the clerks, the social workers and probation officers, the police and the lawyers tend, almost unconsciously, to develop their own 'language network'. There are various phrases and expressions which are a form of shorthand for them; these may be completely incomprehensible to the defendant and parents—and it may seem that things are being said and done from which they are excluded.

At all times, in all these ways, the bench must be careful to see that the proceedings are not passing over the heads of those who have been summoned to the court. That is not only a requirement of the law, but also one of common decency; it is the barest minimum of courtesy at such a time.

Occasionally, even when the defendant has a lawyer there to look after his rights, one must intervene and explain to the defendant what is at issue, for it is not always possible for the lawyer to explain to him what is happening. The case can suddenly be caught up in a tangle of most complicated legal argument which leaves the defendant bewildered. Sometimes, because a situation is testing to the bench and the clerk, and familiar to the lawyer, it may occur to none of them that the defendant sitting in the middle requires to be given some insight into what is being argued and how it affects him and the case.

A court process is not the most natural and simple thing in the world to understand and take part in; nearly everyone comes into a court with some unease or apprehension. It is an important part of the bench's job to allay such tension. The bench may well form opinions on the reliability of various witnesses on either side; it must never allow these to manifest themselves in court through any word, deed, expression or gesture.

The bench, in fact, must provide the calm centre around which the process develops; its own moods, opinions and attitudes must not obtrude into the process. The fact that many members of the public will see this advice being ignored only too frequently in all sorts and levels of courts does not make the advice wrong. Every bench will, on occasion, whether inadvertently or not, fall short of the best standards; nevertheless, it should always be aware of the best standards and aware of its own shortcomings when they appear.

It is the opinionated bench, the emotionally self-indulgent bench, the bench that does not succeed in controlling itself let alone the court, which do harm to the process over which they are called upon to preside. Displays of outrage and anger, of moral righteousness or indignation, usually serve to get in the way of the administration of justice; they may, on occasion, relieve some pressure for any, or all, of the bench—they do no service to the law, nor are they a good basis for proper decision.

The final result sought by the process is the establishment of certain specific facts and a right disposition of a particular case; to establish the facts fully and fairly and arrive at a proper and balanced decision, the emotional temperature of the court should be kept as low as possible. In the 'gladiatorial' tradition of the law, especially when seen in dramatic presentation, it would seem that the generation of tension or stress is somehow conducive to the emergence of truth; I am not sure about truth as an entity in the court process in any case, but I am sure of one thing—in the courts I have sat in through the years I have never seen much that was of use to the court emerge from such situations. Where children and young persons are concerned it is a very dangerous procedure indeed.

A careful, calm and controlled dialogue is much the best way to arrive at the facts and a good decision; the histrionics can be left to dramatic fiction, where they belong.

There are a number of magistrates who will take issue with this point of view. They lay great stress on what they term the dignity of the law. I would not dissent; I have a great regard for the law, but in matters of dignity I think that the dignity of individual human beings takes priority over that of an intellectual concept. The dignity of the law is best safeguarded by ensuring that the dignity of all those engaged in the process is looked to. The maintenance of the true spirit of the law demands this, as I have tried to show.

The bench must not only be the calm centre of the process, it must also be the neutral centre: a little removed from the process, but not above it—apart, but not uninvolved. It has various obligations to which it must pay heed: to the public at large, to the concept of law, and to the people who appear before it. In each individual case it may give due attention to all these different entities, but in the final analysis, it must be concerned most directly with what is most vulnerable in the court—that is, the individuals before it, not least of whom is the defendant. Wrong attitudes or emphases in respect of either of the other entities can be put right or the entities, in the long term, can take care of themselves, but error in respect of the child or young person can result in severe and immediate consequential harm.

6

The Treatment Resources of the Court under the 1969 Act

When the court comes to consider disposal, there are three main courses open to it. The matter is of sufficient importance to warrant a degree of repetition at this point.

The court can bind over the parent or guardian to exercise better control over the child. Alternatively, it can make a Supervision Order. Thirdly, it can make a Care Order to the local authority. There are other alternatives, but these are set out fully in Chapter 2; those mentioned above are the three to which the court usually looks, especially the Supervision and the Care Order.

In addition to making any of these orders, the court has the power to order payment of compensation up to the amount of £100. If the subject is a child, the parents *must* be ordered to pay, and if the subject is a young person, the parents *may* be ordered to pay, only, however, if the court is satisfied that the parent or guardian has contributed to the commission of the offence through failure to exercise proper control or care.

This matter may be argued in court and the parent or guardian must be given a chance to rebut such an allegation. There is also a practical difficulty—most of the families concerned do not command large resources, and orders to pay sums of money of this size could inflict very severe hardship indeed. This is a factor the court has always to bear in mind.

In care proceedings involving young persons, the young person, provided he or she consents, may be bound over to be of good behaviour and keep the peace for a period not exceeding one year; the sum stipulated to ensure good behaviour must not exceed £25.

In criminal proceedings all these forms of disposal are available to the court, along with absolute or conditional discharge, and the imposition of fines. For the moment the court may also make Attendance Centre Orders or Detention Centre Orders, but it is envisaged, under the Act, that when it is fully operative, this power will disappear.

SUPERVISION AND CARE ORDERS

Supervision Orders are not new, but Care Orders were first brought in by the Act.

The Supervision Order places the child or young person under the supervision of the local authority, or the probation service. The court may still choose either, but increasingly, since theirs is the recommending decision, these orders are being made to the local authority, unless that authority suggests the probation service because it is already known by and in contact with the family. The court, in practice, turns more and more frequently to the local authority.

The supervising officer has to 'advise, assist and befriend' the subject of the order. The order may not be made for more than three years, and has various requirements attached to it. One is that the subject shall live with a person named in the order who has agreed to receive him or her. Normally this means in a private household, usually with a relative or friend or some other person who is of significance in the life of the child and who can be of help, for the duration of the order. This is equivalent to the requirement concerning residence under previous Acts which could be imposed in either a Probation Order or a Fit Person Order.

There is one difference: it is no longer necessary by law to obtain the consent of the subject, except in one set of special circumstances. I think, however, it would be an unwise bench which tried to compel a child or young person to live with someone under these circumstances, if there were no indication of consent. The exception is under Section 12(4) of the Act: this is in respect of treatment for mental illness. Here, there is no need for consent from a child, but in the case of a young person the Act states:

> In the case of an order made in respect of a person who has attained the age of fourteen ... [no requirement shall be included] ... unless he consents to its inclusion, and a requirement so included shall not in any case continue in force after the supervised person becomes eighteen.

For the rest, all requirements under supervision orders may now

3

run for the full term of the order, that is, up to a maximum of three years.

The requirement under Section 12(4) is usually resorted to in cases where the mental illness is not of such severity as to warrant detention under a hospital order within the provisions of the Mental Health Act, 1959. The court may order treatment either as an in-patient or as an out-patient in a hospital, but not in a special hospital within the meaning of the 1959 Act. The usual cases in which this is employed arise from drug usage and addiction or dependancy.

Under Section 12(2) of the Act there is a new set of requirements which can be attached to an order, and which have only come into operation during 1973/4. These are concerned with developing 'Intermediate Treatment'. Detailed discussion of this new form of treatment and the problems and opportunities it raises follows in Chapter 10. For the moment, therefore, this mention will suffice. That this new provision is in the Act is important, as is the fact that it is brought into operation through requirements attached to a Supervision Order.

The power of discharging Supervision Orders (Section 15 of the Act) lies with the juvenile court until the supervised person becomes eighteen. Certain special powers are given to the court in the case where the young offender under supervision has reached the age of seventeen and the order was made some time before that age. Those who are concerned with detail can study the Act; such a provision is in the Act to prevent certain anomalies arising in the law when young persons pass from the jurisdiction of the juvenile court and become the concern of the 'adult' court.

To sum up: the Supervision Order partakes of something of the two orders it has replaced—the Supervision Order (old style) and the Probation Order.

The court can also make a Care Order: this is new. The effect of this order is to commit the child or young person to the care of the local authority social services department. It may be made in respect of any child or young person brought before the court under care proceedings, or who has had an offence proved against him which, if committed by an adult, might earn imprisonment.

The duration of a Care Order is determined by the age of the subject when the order is made. If he, or she, is under sixteen the order ends on their eighteenth birthday, unless, because of his or her mental condition or behaviour, the court thinks it should continue for a further year. If, however, the subject is sixteen years or over, the order ends on his nineteenth birthday. In all cases the court has the power to discharge the order at any time before that date, if it thinks fit.

This order supersedes two previous orders of the court; the Fit Person Order and the Approved School Order. It must be made to the local authority where the child or young person lives, if that can be determined; where it cannot, the local authority where the offence took place must undertake responsibility.

The Care Order gives greater flexibility in treating cases. In the past, the court, faced with a child showing disturbed behaviour, had to decide whether it felt it better to place the child with the local authority under a Fit Person Order or send him or her to an Approved School.

Once the order was made the child was categorised, and fitted into a particular compartment of the provision. If, later, it was found that the child sent to an Approved School had emotional problems of such a nature that placement in a school for maladjusteds or some other placement would have been preferable, it was impossible to arrange the move. If it was felt that a child or young person made subject to a Fit Person Order would be better in an Approved School, the authority had to bring the child back to court and make out a case for such a move.

The Care Order gives the local authority very wide powers indeed. Making it does not mean that the child should be removed from home; the subject can, if the local authority decides, remain at home, but the authority does have the power to remove the subject from home and place him or her in a wide range of institutions, if it chooses to do so.

A great deal of the misunderstanding that arose between magistrates and local authorities in the first months of the working of the Act came about because local authorities interpreted the Act strictly in terms of the law; some magistrates had convinced themselves (although it was certainly not in the Act) that when they made a Care Order the local authority would accept this as a direction to remove the child from home and make provision for him or her in some form of institution.

The Act had, in fact, specifically removed that right from the magistrates. It stated that all decisions affecting the future of the child under the order should be taken by the local authority. The social worker responsible can make any reasonable arrangement for the care of the child or young person, which may include removal from home and placement in any one of a number of different establishments, but may also include allowing the child to remain at home and made the subject of care within the community.

An outcry was caused when children under Care Orders and remaining at home were returned to court, charged with further offences.

Many authorities, even if they wished to provide for children away from their own homes, do not command the resources to do so; for others, it was specific policy not to place children in institutions if this could be avoided.

However, if the subjects of Care Orders were to be kept out of further trouble, it meant that the work with them by the social workers had to be of a degree of intensity commensurate with the needs of the order. It became obvious very early on that such close work was neither possible nor forthcoming. Indeed, ironically, many of those under Care Orders seemed to have less supervision and case work than those under Supervision Orders. In the eyes of many children the Care Order, apart from the fact that it could remain in force longer, seemed little different from a Supervision Order—some children treated it as of less consequence.

The concern of the magistrates was that children who needed help were not receiving it. In part this was occasioned by the upheavals of setting up social services departments and by the changes in local authority boundaries; it was also affected by the critical shortage of trained and qualified staff to undertake this task.

That critical position still pertains today; there are many cases where children and young persons subject to Care Orders return to court to plead guilty to a whole string of further offences. There is nothing more the court can do, unless it resorts to ordering detention or recommending Borstal training to those of an age to receive it. This would seem to be a last desperate resort by magistrates concerned to remove a child from home—this would bring relief, possibly to the local community, but might, in fact, merely transfer the problem elsewhere.

If the local authority concludes that it would be better for the child or young person to be removed from home for any period, there are a number of ways in which it can achieve this end. The authority still has powers to board out a subject of an order with a family who are willing to receive him or her, and providing for the child within certain basic limits as required by the authority and established by law. This is a well-tried process for certain children with which the authorities are well familiar.

Alternatively they can place a child or young person in a community home. The community homes, a new description, will comprise former children's homes and some of the old Approved Schools. Community homes will provide for a very wide range of children in need, but it must be remembered that only a very small proportion of them will have arrived there as a result of a court order.

The homes will have residential nursery accommodation for very young children in specialist units; much of the provision will be for children whose own homes have ceased to function or exist. Others will provide training on a par with the old Approved School provision. Others should be concerned with children suffering from specific handicaps and emotional disturbances, and for those who are violent or gravely delinquent, and even provision for those few who are so disturbed that they require a high degree of skill, concentrated staffing and secure provision.

This range should become available to the local authorities under various Regional Plans; at the moment little is available, in sufficient quantity, and the plans show alarming gaps in providing specialist units which will require the greatest concentration of resources. These gaps have a deleterious effect on all attempts at treatment for certain youngsters who come before the courts.

The local authority has power under the provisions of the Act, to make a third type of placement: within a 'voluntary' home. The Act distinguishes between these homes provided by various voluntary bodies and the community homes run by the authorities themselves.

In reality many of these homes will be indistinguishable from community homes, except in the matter of their management. It is hoped that some of the voluntary bodies will make good the worst deficiencies of local authority provision, by establishing small specialist units to deal with particular problems.

The major distinction between community homes and the

voluntary homes provision will be in regard to availability. If a local authority wishes to place a child in its own community homes it will have direct access; if, however, it wishes to place a child in a voluntary home it must convince those responsible for its management that the child or young person is acceptable to the home and can benefit from the provision available. On occasion, when there is a difference of views between the local authority and the receiving home, it may mean that the best placement is not available.

This factor has already created real difficulties in placing certain children; there is no sign that the position is likely to grow any better in the future. In the past, if the court made an Approved School order, that order was backed by statutory provision; the social worker had that much more power in seeking a proper placement. That power is no longer available; as a result some children may have benefited, many more have certainly suffered. Some have not been placed in the establishment which would best have helped them; others have remained at home, under highly unsatisfactory conditions, and many, as a result, have found themselves in more trouble.

There is one important provision in the Act in respect of those subject to care orders; if the child is over five and resident in a community home or any other establishment and has not left the home for more than three months, the local authority must appoint a 'visitor'. This visitor, vetted and appointed by the local authority, has the duty of 'visiting, advising and befriending' the boy or girl, subject to the order, for the duration of the order. This will apply where the child has lost contact with his own home or family, or has none to turn to.

Care Orders may be discharged at any time; the local authority, the parents or guardian, or the 'visitor', where one has been appointed (under section 24(5) of the Act) may apply to the court for the discharge of the order. The power to discharge the order is the only power the court has once the order has been made. The court has no power to interfere nor right to seek consultation with the local authority on how the responsibilities under the order are being discharged.

The effective final decision of the court is made, therefore, when it determines the type of order; when the order is a Care Order there is no more to concern the court, unless the child appears charged with further offences. There is one exception, a process under Section 31 of the Act. This process requires particularly careful scrutiny on the part of the court.

The local authority has the right to apply to the court regarding a young person committed to its care. First it must satisfy the Secretary of State that only by such an application can it provide proper training for the subject of the order in the future. With the permission of the Secretary of State the local authority can apply to the court for a decision under this Section.

The court must then decide whether it is satisfied that the behaviour of the youngster concerned is such that it will be 'detrimental . . . to the person accommodated in any community home for him (or her) to be accommodated there'.

Before this application can be made the youngster must have obtained the age of fifteen, be the subject of a Care Order (but not an interim Care Order), and be accommodated in a community home. The local authority have to make the case that the youngster should be removed to a Borstal institution for training.

If the court so decides then the Care Order is discharged and the subject of the order must be treated as if he, or she, had been sentenced to Borstal training on the date the Care Order was made by the court. This is an extraordinary piece of legislation; it allows the juvenile court to make a decision which is, in effect, a Borstal Order, when it is expressly forbidden to do so under any other circumstances at all. If a juvenile court feels that a young person would benefit from Borstal training, it has to send the child to a higher court with a recommendation to that effect, with no certainty that the recommendation will be carried out.

It is even more extraordinary to find such a provision contained in an Act which removed the power of making an Approved School Order from the court, and also envisages removing the power of making Attendance Centre and Detention Centre Orders from the court in due time. While this has been done, a new power, of a much more drastic sort, has been given to the court, involving young persons presenting the most difficult and exacting sorts of problem.

The cases with which I have had to deal under this section have made me all the more cautious and concerned. In effect, on the recommendation of the local authority, a youngster is removed from a community home straight to Borstal training.

In one such case, every psychiatric report in respect of the girl brought before the court said that Borstal training was contraindicated; the girl, highly intelligent, and approaching seventeen, had made a first-class nuisance of herself (of that there was no doubt) and her life was a total mess. Her plea to the court was that she had grown up, had a boy friend, and wished to make an independent life of her own. She had never committed an offence; she had first come to notice for truancy, and had, in an affection-less way, had a number of boy friends, who were not themselves upright citizens. Much of her trouble arose from the fact that she had no effective family; most of the problems she presented could be found in many more of her age and way of life.

There was no doubt that she had made difficulties for herself and for the various social workers who had tried to help her. There was also, however, some justice in her repeated claims that she was now old enough to make her own mistakes and cope with them. Technically she was in a community home, but her reaction to this attempt to hold her had been so violent that she had spent most of the time in what amounted to solitary confinement, something which made her behaviour worse and more hysterical.

Her behaviour had undoubtedly been unreasonable, but much of it was understandable when a full report of her previous history was read; every conceivable misfortune had struck at her family and her, most of it not of her doing.

The bench, because of the reports which had expressly stated that Borstal training was no answer, were reluctant to find the case proved, which would have had only the one consequence, removal to Borstal. At one time the bench offered to remove the Care Order, but the authority said they would immediately take steps to see that the girl was taken into care again, and the whole process would recommence.

The distressing fact was that, at the end of it all, there was nowhere to deal with a highly intelligent adolescent, with all her special problems, other than by taking a decision which committed her to Borstal, where according to the psychiatric reports, she would be even further damaged. It was a terrifying indictment of the failure to make specialist provision for particularly difficult cases. On that day we refused to make any order, but later we learned that the girl had gone into the hospital wing of Holloway Prison.

Another case was rather similar, involving a boy of fierce independence. He had grown up in one of the London families who make their living in the street markets and follow a way of life which has endured in one form or another for many years. He was brought to court by the social worker. In the course of certain exchanges, the young man said to the social worker, 'I told you, when you first put me in that place [a community home] that I wasn't bloody well going to stay!' He had made good his word over a period of two years. The first error in dealing with the boy had been made on that day, and everything that had happened subsequently had compounded the error.

Again the bench refused to find that a case had been made out that he had been recalcitrant and refused to make any order; instead it suggested to the local authority that some other form of treatment should be tried. The authority, seeing in court how things were between the young man and his social worker, brought in another social worker, who suggested that a hostel might be tried.

This did not succeed, and after several other attempts, the boy was allowed home. The last time I saw him there was a further application before the court from the local authority, to remove the Care Order entirely.

What had happened was interesting. The boy had been placed at home and had seemed to settle into work; there was no father, and he had assumed the role of head of the family, but there had still been difficulties. However, almost without warning, the family were evicted. For the first time, faced with adult responsibility, the boy had responded; he had seen to the rehousing of his family and had conducted himself admirably. The social worker paid full tribute to what he had done; in a very brief time the young man had grown up. We were happy to remove the Care Order and wish him well.

I have given brief details of these two cases to make certain points: first, to draw attention to the gap in provision for difficult, teen-age youngsters, to which I have already made reference. Because of this gap, in both cases, the authority had no other recourse but to turn to Section 31 and Borstal training, as a last resort. Secondly, it was a rare chance for the court to see something of what happened to two youngsters who had been made the subject of Care Orders. In both cases it was obvious that there had been a breakdown in the relationship between the youth and the social worker. In some degree it justified the view of some magistrates that the court has now been too circumscribed in its opportunity to study the working of the Care Order provision. A situation had arisen in both instances between the youngster and the individual social worker which had never been ventilated until the authority had applied to the court under Section 31 of the Act.

The fact was that there was no independent body to intervene between the youngster and the social worker until the situation had passed into crisis. In theory the team-work and reviewing procedure of the local authority should have provided safeguards, but it was obvious, from the attitude of the senior social workers in court, that little had been heard of the youngster's point of view until it emerged in court.

It would be dangerous to make too much of either case, but there are lessons for the court. In both cases the social worker believed that there would be no difficulty in proving that the youngster was recalcitrant, and, indeed, on evidence of behaviour, there was a great deal of material drawn from the files which substantiated such a case. Nor was there much doubt that continuing to live in a community home might well have been detrimental to the other occupants.

The fact was, and I do not apologise for making reference to it once more, that there was no treatment facility available to the local authority which might have coped with these youngsters showing special problems.

More interesting was the fact that neither social worker, in court, was willing to admit the possibility of some error of judgement on their part; one of them reacted with very great indignation when the court put this point of view on behalf of one youngster and complained that the court was going to 'let the youngster off', which would undermine control of all the other difficult youngsters. In only one case had the local authority thought fit to provide representation for the youngster, although they themselves were represented. In the other case the court had to make arrangements and defer the case.

There is a real difficulty here, of course. The local authority has to find someone to represent the youngster whose purpose would be to challenge their assertions and subject their officers to cross-examination. Despite this, it should be done, and the court should ensure that it is done.

In both cases, if the social worker had not been searchingly questioned, the very different picture of the youngster's behaviour would not have emerged—the relationship of the social worker and the youngster was seen in a very different light.

It is important to emphasise that the youngster must be heard and every opportunity given for him or her to challenge the case, and the need for independent representation of the child is critical.

I have been present as an observer in other courts, and have seen cases of this sort dealt with very quickly; there was little scrutiny of the facts, which were accepted as more or less self-evident, and in one case, the unrepresented youngster was hardly listened to at all, and must have got the impression that his point of view was of little interest to the court. Off he went to Borstal, and the outlook did not look good for any further co-operation between him and the social worker.

Ironically, the members of this particular bench were vociferous in complaining about their lost right to make Approved School Orders.

We are in a very difficult field of concern. While, strictly, it was never the courts' function to do anything about the provision made for treatment, most magistrates, made aware of the needs of the children and young persons who appeared before them, played an honourable part in developing forms of treatment and new approaches to children and young people in trouble. Perhaps some of them were resented in the past.

There is no doubt that the outcry raised by certain magistrates during the passing of the Bill and the first months of the working of the Act aroused a degree of suspicion on the part of the social workers. It would be regrettable if this were to continue.

There is increasing need of close liaison between the court and the social services, between the magistrates and social workers, and the Act, in fact, calls for this. A new form of relationship must be established; the bench must accept its role, and understand it clearly: it is just as important for the social workers to understand the role of the magistrates. That each will scrutinise the other and be critical at all times is fundamental to the working of the Act.

Critical scrutiny on both sides should not preclude communication; new ways of developing exchanges of views and experience must be developed, so that the wide area of common concern can be explored to mutual advantage.

I would hope, as everyone grows more accustomed to the working of the Act, and when the Act's provisions are fully implemented, that confidence will grow on both sides. In the past the magistrates and the local authorities were allies in the battle to develop more understanding in the general community and to make more resources available for the treatment of those who were their common concern; in the future they will need one another even more.

7

The Social Worker and the Court

The most valuable resource that the court has available to it is the individual social worker and the teams of workers within the local authority social services departments. The social worker, supplying reports to the court, assuming responsibility under the Act for the treatment of children and young persons is the key to its successful working.

I have had wide contacts with social workers in all sorts of settings and with many different functions and responsibilities over many years; I have joined with them in working parties, discussion groups, work situations and conferences over fairly extensive periods; I have also been involved in various ways with the training of social workers: but I am not a social worker and can only speak of them and their role from an outside point of view.

Their main job is not to do with courts at all, so there is a danger of a wrong emphasis in all that I say. Every social worker has a particular group of people whom they have to help, befriend and sustain. Their key task is to develop relationships of trust, usefulness and understanding with these people, whom they describe as their 'clients'.

A number of social workers feel uneasy about the use of the word 'client' in their particular context. Lawyers have clients in the courts; but is the relationship between a lawyer and his client comparable in any way with the relationship of the social worker and his, or her, 'client'? However, for reasons of portmanteau-convenience, the use of the word seems to have become widespread, and I will therefore adopt it.

Some social workers, for reasons which they feel are good (some of which I understand, and a few of which I sympathise with), dislike certain aspects of the court process. Some few dislike the courts entirely, and feel that they are an unnecessary intrusion into the organisation of good social work. There are some who maintain that the courts are positively harmful.

My own view is that the court is a necessary part in the function of providing care and assessing treatment for children and young persons in conflict with society and the law. The capacity of the court to scrutinise both the police and the social worker in their tasks is important. I cannot draw any distinction between the necessity to scrutinise one or the other.

It is equally important for the social workers to maintain a close scrutiny of the court and develop an understanding of what takes place there. Social workers must study the ways in which a court goes about making decisions and the grounds on which those decisions are made, especially since their reports will be a major influence at various stages in the court process.

I have quoted one or two unkind 'stereotypes' created by some magistrates when looking at social workers. Social workers also have their stereotype of the magistrate. The most eloquent I have heard was made by a Welshman: 'Puffed-up, jumped-up, repressed punishers with a degree of self-importance matched only by their ignorance.'

Magistrates, on the whole, are much less interesting than this! It is always instructive, however, to look at stereotypes and try to discover what went into making them. They represent the crystallisation of resentment and prejudice, and indicate possible areas of misunderstanding and discord.

These mutually destructive views of one another have emerged because of the peculiar circumstances of the last few years. Many present-day social workers are young, particularly those the magistrates tend to meet in court.

The social services' departments have faced many problems since their inception in 1970, one of which has been recruitment. With the expansion of work in the social services' field, social work has become a 'growth' industry.

Many of the workers who had been in the field for years in various capacities found senior posts in the new departments: this removed them from direct contact with 'clients' and the courts. Their new posts were administrative, supervisory and supportive. The day-to-day work, the immediate and direct contact with clients was left to the new entrants, who were, in the nature of things, mostly young and, to a degree, lacking in experience.

I am not implying that the social services' departments recruited inferior people to fill the gaps at lower levels; they have rightly maintained very high standards, and the qualifications and professional training of the entrants has never been higher. The various bodies concerned with training, recruitment and the professional standing of social workers have ensured this. But it did happen, in newly formed departments, many younger workers were having to cope with new pressures and stresses in a field which itself was only being defined as they worked in it.

These younger workers were learning their job, in practice as opposed to theory, at a time when the pressures upon them were very great and the framework of support and supervision was itself under greatest stress. Many of them had problems of their own, some personal, some in connection with the work they were called upon to undertake. Working through these problems will, in the end, make them more valuable members of the social work team, as they gain experience. Their mood, refreshingly, was to question everything and to accept nothing on face value, including themselves and their qualifications, over the whole range of their responsibilities, and to question their role both in their departments and society.

They belong to a generation which looks hard and long at all authority, and distrusts authoritarian and paternalistic attitudes. They suspect what they call the Establishment, and for them the Establishment has many faces and reveals itself in many ways and places; many of them see the courts and all those who have anything to do with the courts as part of the Establishment, part of a manipulating and controlling society.

Their identification with their 'clients' leads them to be against all such establishment manifestations. For this reason the stereotype magistrate and the stereotype policeman are necessary to them; they can focus their dislike and distrust on the stereotypes, without examining reality too closely. For a small, but significant, number, this dislike and distrust comes close to dismissive hatred, because, in part, the real dislike and distrust is of themselves for having to exercise control and use manipulative skills in carrying out their own job.

The dislike focuses upon the court, and in particular the magistrates and the police, because it is in the court situation that social workers are called upon to face this other side of their own role that they would wish to ignore; they emphasise the negative aspect in an attempt to disassociate themselves from an aspect of their work which causes them concern and heart-searching—and for this reason, their reaction can sometimes be all the fiercer.

If mutual scrutiny cannot pass beyond an initial antagonism and rejection, it can be very destructive. The relationship between magistrates and social workers needs careful tending from both sides; it should be possible to establish common ground from differing standpoints. Negative postures of disapproval or dislike may give a certain temporary satisfaction (to either side), but the people who suffer are those whom both groups are really concerned to help.

In a series of extended examinations of these feelings over a number of meetings, some interesting points of view emerged. To many social workers the court was a closed community, which some of them thought of as much more powerful than in fact it is.

It soon became apparent that many of the social workers did not know how the court worked, what its powers were, nor what its precise functions were, nor how they changed from stage to stage of the proceedings. Since the court represented alien territory and drew upon long-established traditions which had become somewhat ritualised, and process seemed empty of meaning to many of them, and lacking in content in ways which aroused their suspicions and mistrust.

A number of them believed that courts existed only 'to send people away', and that magistrates had only this one role and were lusting to carry it out. They could not accept that magistrates were as concerned and often as baffled as they were; they needed authoritarian figures to react against, and the court seemed to offer them. Their view of the magistrate did not include that concern for the welfare of the child which has been laid upon the court as a first consideration for many years. Many of them felt that the court was outside the scope of their proper concerns and occasionally restricting their proper function.

To most of them, courts meant trouble. This is true. It meant that their clients were in trouble, and that they would be put to all sorts of trouble, both in the courts and afterwards. It also meant that there was likely to be some scrutiny of their way of dealing with a particular client.

They were also very sensitive to the anomalous position in which they might find themselves in the court itself. This sensitivity derived partly from their fear of courts. They had little understanding of how they might effectively join in the court process to help their clients.

With one group, a simple exposition of who was in the court, where the magistrates sat, where the clerk sat, where the social workers sat, where the probation officers sat, where the lawyers sat, seemed to be helpful. Further explanation of what was going on, how the court should be addressed and the nature of the process, aroused considerable interest. This was followed by observational visits to the courts. As a result, much of the early uneasiness disappeared, and it seemed fair to assume that what is not known is mistrusted.

Those who participated in a 'role-playing' exercise set in a court said afterwards that on their next appearance in court they felt much more at ease and believed they were more effective, not only in making their reports but putting their point of view on behalf of clients. All of them agreed that with their growing understanding of the court they were likely to be of much greater service both to the court and their clients.

In fact, when their clients get into trouble with the law, it is an obligation upon them to know about the court and its procedure; they are in the best position to give first-hand advice to their clients about their rights before they answer the summons. They can also explain the legal aid service and ensure that their clients are properly represented when they first come to court.

None of this is possible if the social worker, for whatever reason, pretends that the court is not there, or that if he waits long enough it will go away or disappear. He may believe passionately that it should not be there, or wish for it to disappear, but while it is there and his clients are likely to appear in it, he should do all he can to learn about it, gain experience of it and be the first line of support and guidance to his clients when they do appear.

The social worker's involvement with a case will begin before the bench's. The police and local authority will have consulted on the need to issue a summons in the first place; the local authority will have been informed (except in very rare instances) and should have considered whether, under the terms of the Act, a summons should be issued or some other procedure adopted. The social worker can help his clients and their families at this stage, and good advice may save a number of appearances in court and long adjournments.

Whether the social worker wants to be involved with the legal system or not, there is no doubt that, from time to time, he, or she, will be. The probation officer had a well recognised role in the court; the social worker must now assume that role. The fact that many social workers never envisaged court work as part of their responsibility has no validity in the light of the very specific functions that the 1969 Act lays upon the social services departments of the local authority. They have been given a central role in the working of the Act and they must be prepared to assume it fully.

There is no doubt that any court of law is a formidable place; it embodies a legalistic attitude which is in sharp contrast with the attitudes that the social worker seeks to cultivate.

The social workers carry out their duties with a respect for the individual. I have tried to show that the court, in its own fashion, has to do likewise. It has to respect the dignity of all those who come before it, and its prime function is the protection of individual rights. Many social workers do not see these claims on behalf of the court as valid. Some of them have had bad experiences of courts, and others, because of a general philosophy of society, will not admit this concern on the part of the court.

Many social workers see the court's function as very narrow— the protection of society against aberrant individuals who are likely to offend against its standards and attitudes. This is one of the duties of the court, but, as I have tried to show, it is balanced against others, including the needs of the individual.

Confidentiality is another matter of concern to the social worker. The court seems to infringe upon this in discussing reports, possibly (from the social worker's point of view) misusing reports to prove certain matters against the client, calling into account material which was gathered in the first place under conditions of trust. That the social worker has very real problems in this area of relationship with the client can make his or her resentment towards the court all the more pointed.

The social worker also has two other ideals: to be non-judging, or, at least, non-condemnatory, is one; to maintain non-directiveness, is the other. The legal process would seem to run counter to both of these; the court must be concerned with judgement, and takes decisions which intervene directly in the lives of many individuals.

I hope that these brief summaries do not caricature certain social work attitudes. No one will pretend that these are not worthy ideals. Like most ideals they are guiding principles which, in an imperfect world full of ordinary people, are necessarily compromised from time to time. There are very few social workers who can live up to them on all occasions, because the categories of moral attitude are not so easily soluble.

We have come to the perennial dilemma—mad or bad? Is every manifestation of unacceptable behaviour to be seen finally as some form of sickness, or is such behaviour a symptom of an underlying sickness in the whole society? Most people will have some sympathy with these points of view. They will not necessarily want to see these attitudes, or their contraries, taken to an extreme.

There are the rights of individuals, particularly sick individuals, to be safeguarded; there are also the rights of the individuals who suffer as a result of their behaviour—these also must receive attention and respect. In the real world all sorts of individuals are having to strike uneasy balances between conflicting rights.

When we come to the rights of the individuals who are likely to be the concern either of the courts or the social workers the matter is even more subtle and searching. It may be convenient for some workers to think in terms of ill-health; this leaves very little dignity to the client. It is denying the client the respect that society gives him in holding him (or her) responsible for their behaviour, or being capable of rational moral decision, and of foreseeing the consequences of actions.

Very often the social worker denies dignity to the client under the guise of benevolent concern; sometimes the client is subjected to far more manipulation of his life than can arise from a confrontation with the court with its simple categories of guilt and innocence. Indeed the manipulative coercion of the social worker may be far more corrosive of individual rights and freedom, on occasion, than the more open approach of the court, which, with all its ritual, grants the client the dignity of responsibility, if only as a defendant.

While these problems are the concern of the bench and all other agencies of the court (not least the police, although their emphasis is different) they are particularly critical and poignant for the social worker, for they go to the heart of the social worker's role, but they are questions that concern others also, and it is unfortunate that some social workers assume that they are the only guardians of these particular ideals.

I have referred to the openness of the court process: a specific allegation is made, facts are produced and examined, and an assessment of the future is attempted. At every stage, the defendant is consulted and represented. A similar process takes place in the social work agency; very often it is much less open. Allegations, though not in such specific terms, are made, facts adduced, and decisions taken—the fact that they are described as social enquiry, diagnosis and treatment does not, in fact, materially alter the reality. While clients are consulted at the early stage and listened to with great patience and understanding, it is fair to put certain questions: How often are they told in specific terms of the nature of the allegation made against them? How much opportunity do they have to give observations upon the diagnosis? How much part do they play in discussing and possibly rebutting the reports? Is their voice heard about the decisions respecting treatment?

I laid great stress on the need to explain continually to the defendant, in the court context, what is happening, and what his, or her, rights are, and the need to ensure that adequate representation of those views is given to the court. How much explanation of this kind, particularly as to rights vis-à-vis the social agency as opposed to rights vis-à-vis other agencies, takes place within the social work process?

I do not know. The questions need to be asked. Not in an unfriendly or challenging spirit, but because they are important. Some workers make assumptions about the court process which, in fact, might be made by others about their own process. Their code of ethics, their professional standards and their individual sensitivity and scrupulousness are not in question; they should not disregard the same standards of care and concern in others.

To many social workers there seems an awful inevitability about the legal process, once it has begun to move in a particular case; there are, at each step, certain safeguards, and their own intervention can do much to make the result sensitive and responsive to the needs of their clients. Similarly there can be an awful inevitability about their own process once a 'case' has come to attention, and there are not many statutory checks or safeguards or, at least, not many so conspicuously written into the process nor subject to scrutiny so often.

The opportunity for the social worker within the court process is very far-reaching. In the antagonistic concept of judicial process, the court is like an arena; an arena used by professionals, by lawyers and police. Social workers must acquire the same professional status (derived from their own discipline) in the court; they must learn to match their professional skills with others'. They are professionals of a very special kind, with a very special place in the process; they can influence the decisions of the court and the decisions as to treatment more directly and more powerfully than any other professional present in court.

There are certain matters which enhance or detract from this professional standing within the court context. One of them is an occasional over-identification with the client-defendant. Over-close identification, to the point where other interests are scorned or treated as illegitimate, can be counter-productive and result in possible harm to the client's interests.

The public scrutiny of what is said by the social worker is no more pleasurable for them than it is for the police, or any other witness, or the court—yet all are subject to it. The fact that the social worker must be prepared to undergo cross-examination and be able to substantiate what he says is a useful reminder of the discipline he should always follow in recording fact and observation.

That their observation and deductions can be challenged not only by the lawyers in the court, but by the bench and the client/defendant is sometimes a shock to some social workers. They must learn to ride this shock and be prepared to go into the public arena in this fashion, for much of their effectiveness and much of their status as a body of professional workers is receiving examination on such occasions.

Speculation can sometimes creep into reports; also, regrettably, gossip. All social workers know only too well that this is wrong: yet I have read reports where the kindest description of certain passages would have been gossip—less kindly, at times, it could have been seen as vindictiveness towards some other party, in misguided zeal for their client or their own point of view.

In one such report, concerned with whether a mother was a fit person to continue caring for a child, two assertions were made about the mother—that she drank and that she might well be a part-time prostitute. This, as is sometimes the practice in reports to the juvenile court, was marked by an inked line in red down the side of these remarks. This indicated that they might be 'sensitive' material; in the bench's view, they were also of critical importance.

There seemed no way to put these points to the mother in any summarised fashion, but at the same time the child standing alongside the mother in front of the bench had to be considered. The bench asked the child to leave court. The allegations were then put to the mother. She vigorously denied them, and asked the social worker what evidence she had. None seemed to be forthcoming from direct observation. The mother then told the social worker which of her neighbours in the block of flats would have made these allegations. The social worker's face showed that the mother had scored a hit. In the end, after an embarrassing scene, the social worker had to admit there was no evidence that the mother drank and withdrew completely any allegation that she was a part-time prostitute.

When the child came back into court the bench informed her that certain matters affecting her mother had been discussed in her absence, and that, now they were cleared up, the bench was not taking them into consideration in coming to a decision. The law requires the child to be informed, but the terms of what we told the child were agreed with the mother before the child returned.

This anecdote illustrates once more the need for care on the part of the court, and also on the part of the individual social worker. It also emphasises the need to understand what is evidence, what is hearsay and, regrettably in this case, what is gossip. I know that such a report would not have been presented in these terms by a more experienced social worker, and is far from typical; it must be treated as an extreme aberration, but useful as an illustration of some of the difficulties and dangers, and the need for some form of scrutiny of reports.

Subsequently the bench did discuss this particular case with the social services department; it was treated seriously by both sides, but recognised as an isolated error in this extreme form. Nevertheless, such an incident does raise questions about material that goes into reports on which decisions are taken when they are not subjected to such scrutiny.

What was disturbing was the fact that the social worker, fired with the need to help a particular child in what was seen as damaging circumstances, had not respected the rights and dignity of the mother, and had moved from a non-judgemental attitude into a condemnatory stance—in the belief that this was the best way to help the child.

At subsequent discussions the social worker complained of the breach of confidentiality, saying it was now impossible to work with the mother because of the exchanges that had taken place in court.

This seemed to weigh more with the social worker than the damage the mother could have sustained if certain allegations in the report had gone unchallenged. The social worker deplored the fact that the court had not been able to issue an order for proper provision to be made for the child. But this can never be made on the basis of gossip or wrong facts; and much as the bench may sympathise with the aims of social work, it cannot connive at false evidence. If it did so in respect of any other agency in the court, say, the police, the social workers would be the first to complain.

These matters have not been raised to attack social workers or their service, but to illustrate some of the difficulties that arise. Nothing I have said should be viewed negatively; it is meant to be constructive. The court is so dependent upon the social worker, that it must be able to place complete reliance on his integrity, professional skill and good judgement at all times, or the system will fail.

Under the new Act the court has little power beyond licensing the social worker to proceed with some form of treatment. The real power, and it is quite awesome, is now with the social services department and the individual social worker. They can devise methods of treatment and intervene in the lives of children, young persons and their families in ways which have never been possible to a court.

The individual social worker is responsible to the area-, group- or team-leader, and, subject for most of the time to the scrutiny of their own department and their own professional skill and individual conscience, can decide to remove a child from home or leave him in his home, and take many other actions which impinge upon the life of the child or young person more directly than any order of the court.

Many social workers fall back on the case conference, which is part of their method of working, which provides their own form of scrutiny. Whoever else may be at that conference, from all I have been able to discover, very rarely, if at all, will the client be there. Indeed many social workers take the view that it would not be professional for this to happen. This is in sharp contrast to the court situation, where the client/defendant must be present and can challenge anything or everything said about him or her.

The court experience, where the client has more voice, is important for social workers; it should refresh their own insights and sharpen their professional reflexes. It can also serve to suggest other forms of question than those they must continually put to themselves about their role and the individual disposition of cases.

Part of the social workers' role involves them with the court. Social workers are one particular source of insight, understanding and information, invaluable to the court. They are not supermen and women, but professional people, using their skill to the best level they know how, subject to their own questioning and uncertainty, but unique in that they have a more direct, deeper and more fully rounded picture of the client/defendant than anyone else in court. In turn, the bench is as uncertain, confused and concerned as they, working from the standpoint of lay men and women, without particular professional skill, but deploying such insight as their experience has given them. Each needs the other.

The social worker can share his insight, understanding and compassion, his knowledge of the resources available and the particular hopes for a particular client with the court. Social workers can be a sensitising and informing agent in the court. The court must make a decision; the social worker can offer his knowledge, consistent ethics and responsibility to make that decision the best possible.

To achieve this the social workers must understand the court, know how to present their reports, and serve their information to the court in the best fashion: this entails studying how the court works, what it can do, and learning how to intervene most effectively in the working of the court. Social workers owe this to their clients, the court, themselves, and, not least, their profession.

8

Residential Care

The impact of the Seebohm Committee's recommendations and their implementation through the Local Authority Social Services Act, 1970, have already been referred to. The Children & Young Persons Act, 1969, had been devised on an earlier assumption that the experienced body of workers who had gathered together in Children's Departments in the local authorities would be available to implement the Act. As a result of the arrival of the Social Services Act on the statute book, this did not happen. Most of the trained workers remained available, but their attention was directed towards other groups, and their skills were diffused.

Seebohm sought to bring about a degree of rationalisation and to provide a much more comprehensive service in an effort to overcome the previous fragmentation of responsibility which had been occasioned through the piecemeal development of the Social Services, spread through various departments of local government and other agencies.

A degree of unification was achieved by the Act; the Social Services absorbed the work of the Children's and Welfare Departments, and those functions of the Health departments which, in the view of the Seebohm Committee, had primarily a social work content. This left a larger part of social work outside the Social Services Departments: most notably, the probation service, social work in hospitals, the educational welfare service and most Child Guidance work.

A totally integrated service was not possible. There still remains confusion as to responsibility in certain areas, especially among people using the services, and there are still boundary disputes, areas of overlapping which create interdepartmental rivalry, and a number of gaps. The new departments resolved some of the old disputes and removed certain areas of difficult relationships, only to reveal fresh ones.

The new, more comprehensive service was intended to 'reach

far beyond the discovery and rescue of social casualties'. It was
to play a new role in the community, working for the community's
overall social health. Its other work was to deal with those immediately at risk because of some unforeseen crisis.

The service was to become less of a 'fire-brigade', rushing in
to deal with particular crisis situations, and was to concentrate
on developing social strategies and policies to prevent family
and individual breakdown, rather than cure these conditions
once they had occurred.

In the event the many new responsibilities placed upon the
departments have meant that most of them are working more as
'fire-brigades' today than in the past. There have been few opportunities to stand back from the immediate crises to study the
wider considerations and develop the preventive work which was
to be the chief gain from the larger, more comprehensive organisation.

Most Social Services Departments have been under such pressure because increased work, staff shortages and crises of role
that many of their priority groups have tended to recede from
immediate attention. This has certainly happened in some measure
in the field of child-care; under the Children's Departments
those children in need and their families had a body of workers
who gave undivided attention to their particular problems.
Children and young persons have now moved from the head of
their own particular queue a long way back in the queue that
formed when the Social Services Departments came into being.
If the new departments were supposed to look at the child in the
more comprehensive setting of the family, and devise more
imaginative and sensitive responses to problems and needs, for
the most part this has failed to happen.

In the newly formed departments workers were brought
together from very different backgrounds and with differing
interests, senses of priority and skills; some were formally trained,
others were not. Most of them have worked in a narrower field
than they were now called upon to cover; for some the main
concern had been children in need and their families; others had
worked with old people and the handicapped; still others had
been concerned with the inadequate or the mentally ill. They
became members of working teams in departments where all
these problems were likely to present themselves, and they were
expected to deal with a cross-section of all the problems put before

them. For most of them it meant acquiring new insights, new areas of sensitivity, and modified skills; because of the pressure of work, many of them had to acquire these insights and skills within the department while continuing at their work.

New entrants to the departments had received 'generic' training: this was more generalised than the previous training directed to specific groups, needs and problems. Necessarily such training has been concerned more with 'attitudes' and less with specific practical techniques, and was to a degree more diffuse. The attitudes which have emerged in the workers trained under this new system are important, and some of them are in sharp contrast to those of some of the older, more experienced workers.

In some Social Services Departments there is such a sharp division in attitudes that, in a number of instances, it militates against the coherent working of the system. No doubt, in time, such internal conflicts will sort themselves out through the system; they will probably result in better systems of working and more rational deployment of skills. In the meantime there is a certain loss of service to clients, while these issues remain unresolved.

The largest part of all social work in the past was case-work, which was problem-orientated. Two other forms of social work, group-work and community-work, had not received sufficient emphasis or attention. Some group-work had been attempted, through various agencies, but this had primarily been confined to work with children and young people, and the old—this is now receiving much more attention and is being widened in scope and application.

Community work, which has a long pedigree, had received little attention from local authorities under the old division of responsibility, is now being developed, but because of pressure seems to be confined largely to problem areas.

All these forms of social work were carried on by what might be termed the 'field' workers; the other broad category of social work is residential care, and this, as it applies to children and young persons, is one of our main concerns. The newly trained social workers, in particular, have ambivalent attitudes towards residential care. Their training tends to make them look on it as the least satisfactory form of provision. Many of them are trained to see it as a policy of last resort.

Such an attitude reflects that towards the whole field of provision for children (and other groups) for the last few decades.

The major emphasis has increasingly been on work in the community and the avoidance of institutionalisation. This is necessary and desirable, but it has had one unfortunate effect: the people responsible for residential care now feel that their contribution has been downgraded, and is constantly under attack. They feel that their role, which is very demanding, has received too little attention, not enough appreciation and too little regard.

It is noticeable also that highly trained workers choose not to go into residential work. This means that the percolation of new ideas, new approaches and new insights has been less effective in the residential context, so that again residential workers feel they suffer a loss of esteem. There has been a serious loss of morale in residential work, even though that role is still necessary (even if in a diminished form) in caring for children and providing for certain children in difficulties. A noticeable rift has developed between field and residential workers.

Complaints about each side from the other can be gathered very easily, with no prompting; both sides feel that the other lacks understanding of their particular role. In the end there has been a loss of quality in general provision of care.

There is need for much more and much higher standards of professional training for residential staff, with the creation of many more opportunities for developing their role and widening the professional basis of their work. More effort must be made to give residential workers access to more specialised and highly qualified skills from the psychiatric and psychological services. Because of loss of esteem and falling levels of recruitment consequent in part on that loss of esteem, that part of the service which is still of great importance is on a downward spiral, and vigorous action is necessary to reverse the trend.

Residential work is exacting; it calls for special skills and particular dedication; it demands an involvement in the lives of individual children and young people at moments of stress and confusion of a degree which the field workers seldom experience or can enter into with anything like the same degree of intimacy or intensity. Residential workers are always on call whilst in the establishment, and their hours are necessarily long. Many of them are hurt and bewildered by the attitude of those whom they look upon as their colleagues in the field, who seem not to value their work or appreciate their skills.

'When they come here it's like an inspection. They behave as if they're not part of the same organisation, to hear them talk. They want to give us orders.'

'They talk about their kids. The kids don't know them, and they don't know the kids. They've never seen them going to bed, and they've never seen them trying to hide wet sheets when they get up in the morning!'

The residential workers contrast their own long hours with the hours they believe the field workers put in. 'Try to reach them before ten o'clock in the morning or after four o'clock in the afternoon! You can never get them. They're never there. And in any case, they don't want to talk to us. They don't think we have anything important to say to them.'

There is a lack of communication on both sides in some instances which is truly alarming. The residential workers may wish to know more of the child's home and background, but they complain that the field workers do not treat them as professional equals, and try to decide what information they should be given and what should be withheld. Each side has its own view of the child: it is often difficult for the two views to be brought together and reconciled. The result is a degree of frustration which can only be harmful.

There seems little ill-will in this situation; it arises from a 'professional' stance on the one side, which strikes the residential worker as cold and aloof, and which reinforces the residential workers' feeling that their knowledge, insight and capacities are undervalued, if not totally disregarded.

The roots of this misunderstanding lie far back in the history of social provision. Residential care derives from the days of the Poor Law and the charitable foundations of the Victorian era; it still carries overtones from that time in the minds of many social workers.

The training of the social worker imbues him or her with the belief that removing a child from home is a major failure (and for most of the time most people would agree). Residential workers are coping with the children the field social workers have been unable to help, at the end of a series of failures on the part of home, parents, school and school community, and the wider community as a whole. But for many field social workers a degree of responsibility attaches to them which they cannot easily accept or live with professionally. The residential establishment represents their failure, and this colours their attitude to some of them.

In the past the ready resort for all difficulties with children was placement away from home, in a residential establishment; it is healthy that a reaction against this solution (which was not a real solution in many cases) had developed. There are still, however, in the community, a number of children, so damaged and confused, that there is no help available to them other than in a residential setting. However much we deplore this, and however much more we may do in the future to try to prevent this, within the foreseeable future, the need for provision of this sort is likely to continue. Even if it is the solution of last resort, it is necessary to have it.

Indeed, the greater discrimination in recommending residential placement has meant that the children now requiring help in a residential setting present more serious and searching problems than in the past. This means that the call upon the skills and professional expertise of those working within the establishments has become more challenging and diverse. In fact, with the loss of prestige of this type of work, training for residential staff has languished, while training for other forms of work has received far more attention and far more investment; training for residential staff should have kept pace, at least, and there is a good case for giving it a degree of priority which it has yet to receive.

Residential staff need more professional support and a greater volume of expert advice and guidance than is available to them at the moment. They are so fully occupied with the problems of their immediate involvement that they feel they have been left in isolation from the mainstream of social work and training. They feel an urgent need to know what is going on, and to be informed of new developments taking place in the service, and they look for a much deeper understanding of the new problems they are being called upon to cope with.

In the past each establishment would have its own management committee; many now are administered from the local government offices. The staff feel once more that they no longer have anyone directly interested in their own establishment and its problems to turn to, and again their sense of isolation is increased. This feeling, whether real or imagined, cannot be good for morale, and cannot be good for the quality of child care offered. It means that little development can occur either for the staff or the children they are responsible for.

It is often touching to observe residential workers' desire for guidance and advice, for commendation and assessment of their role, from anyone who comes from the world 'outside'—many of them now think in these terms, which in any view cannot be healthy.

It is difficult for them to find the necessary devotion for a task which many of their professional colleagues affect to despise; surprisingly that devotion is still evident in large measure. But numbers of the better and more promising young staff who come into this work soon realise that the rewards are greater in other areas of social work, and the demands less exacting, and quickly move on, so the staff shortages are made worse by the loss of some of the best and most enthusiastic staff.

The irony is, as I have already indicated, that the processes of the working of the Children & Young Persons Act make increasing demands upon that devotion, especially in the case of severely disturbed children.

With so many safety nets now spread to prevent children getting into trouble, or into more serious trouble, and so many devices adopted to prevent removal from the home community, the children who finally arrive in these establishments via the courts and a Care Order, are so much more damaged, so much more desperate that they present problems of a degree of intensity greater than in the past.

To deal with these disturbed children we now have a service whose morale is low, whose recruitment problems are worsening, and whose standards of professional training and status have remained depressed while other sectors have advanced. There are modes and fashions in social work as in all other forms of activity—and the present mode is to undervalue the role of the residential worker.

A better pay structure might lead to better staffing ratios, and a full use of resources, and present the establishments with more opportunity to develop training and clarify their role and long-term future. If the pressure were eased in some areas, the opportunity of broadening the outlook of residential staff would be of immense value. But, as one training officer put it, if we arrange courses for our residential staff, they go off and then are subjected to a barrage of criticism about their role and return either depressed and dispirited or seek work in some other area of social work and are lost to us.

Willingness to use residential provision varies from authority to authority, as once it varied from court area to court area. The initial period, after the first parts of the Act were implemented, and when there was a marked reluctance to use such provision, has been followed by a greater recourse to this particular resource. But there are still considerable variations, not only from one authority to another, but within the authority's Social Services Department itself.

Part of this variation arises from the unequal geographical distribution of the old Approved Schools, which have continued as Community Homes, their new title under the Act. Most authorities are reluctant to place children in establishments a long way from their own home.

The greatest difficulty is to place specially difficult children. In part, this stems from the reluctance of many of the Community Homes to persist in their efforts to help a difficult child; they have problems of staffing and loss of morale to contend with, as I have indicated. This means that if a child presents serious problems and persists in running away, the Community Home will lose patience and request removal of the child. It then becomes very difficult to find another Community Home willing to take on such a child: as one admissions officer put it to me, 'Why, with their own problems, should they buy more grief?'

The result is that the child who is possibly more in need of some form of residential provision than many others who have conformed and remained in their original placement, will be returned home, to the circumstances which contributed to his or her original difficulties, and more serious trouble will result.

The unfortunate consequence of this has been the reaction of some of the courts; they have resorted to the use of Detention Centre Orders or Borstal training to provide some form of containment for young people they felt were at risk, or were a risk to the community.

The changes the Act brought about have created this situation. Previously the statutory requirement that the subject of an Approved School Order had to be placed in an Approved School, called upon the Secretary of State for Home Affairs, working through the Home Office Inspectorate, to see that the order would be carried out.

In the past, when the subject of an order was causing difficulties in a particular school, or absconding frequently, there was the realistic possibility of placement in another school. But those responsible for admission to the ex-Approved Schools are more reluctant today to take a child back when he has absconded, because of the unsettling effect such a child has, and other schools are less likely to receive him on transfer. Many schools choose to play safe, and refuse such youngsters in the first place, so that they are never faced with the problem at all.

This has meant a clogging up of Remand Homes, Assessment Centres and Reception Centres, and an accumulation in those establishments of some of the most troublesome children, who make the running of the place that much more difficult.

For some of the inner-urban areas, notably London, this has now become a grave problem. Certain children, presenting the most difficult problems of behaviour, cannot be placed at all.

A boy of fifteen who assaulted staff in an Assessment Centre so badly that he had to be transferred to a Remand Centre was finally sent to a Detention Centre. Part of the report on him read as follows: 'A boy who could benefit from being committed to care and placed in an appropriate Community Home. Unfortunately, of the six schools available to this region for boys of his age, two are full and have no sign of a vacancy, two are closing or changing management and have not sufficient staff to cope with a boy of this temperament and type of problem, and the two others would not accept him.'

A fifteen-year-old girl, 'the focus of her mother's hostility', ran away from home in January and was subsequently taken into care because of her mother's attitude towards her. In March a case conference decided that 'Because of her growing aggression and uncontrolled behaviour towards other children and adults' she be found a place in a Community Home. There was no place available and she continued in a Reception Centre, going out to school, but was excluded from school because of an attack on a teacher in May. In July a further serious assault on a member of the Reception Centre staff caused grave concern. This was followed by a series of assaults on children and other staff, and running away until October. While absconding she was arrested for theft and assault, but no remand place was available and she was returned to the children's Reception Centre. By November this could not contain her any longer, and 'failing any other placement' she was remanded to Holloway for one week. A Remand Centre placement was then found for her for a further fortnight, but at the other end of England: finally she had to

4

return to the Reception Centre where her pattern of unsatisfactory behaviour continued.

The following January the social worker reported, after a further case conference, 'We still believe that she would be best accommodated in a Community Home,' but there was no place anywhere, in any Community Home, available to her.

These are only two of many such cases, chosen because they illustrate some of the difficulties. The effect of a small number of children of this sort is not to be measured statistically. They cause disruption in schools, Reception Centres, Assessment Centres and Remand Homes and any other establishment which tries to help them. They demand an excessive amount of time from the staff, which means that the needs of other children are neglected and their lives made more miserable during a period of stress in their own development. The consequent blight on the lives of many other children and members of staff which follows upon trying to contain these difficult children in places which are not staffed nor equipped to help them is serious.

It was thought that some of these cases, presenting apparently serious mental problems, might be accommodated in the adolescent units attached to certain mental hospitals. Such places are themselves in very short supply, but they do, in theory, have access to greater skills in dealing with certain aspects of such problems. The hospitals, however, seem very reluctant to receive these specially difficult children.

A girl of fifteen, who was 'seriously emotionally deprived', and was possibly educationally subnormal, and who showed signs of increasing aggression towards others and towards herself, was treated for two years in an adolescent unit. During that time she showed increased tendencies towards violence and suicide. In the end the hospital said 'It was no longer able to contain her'. She then appeared in the juvenile court again, and the court was told by the social worker, 'I do not know of any Community Home which would accept her'.

The search for some sort of accommodation continued for a long time, and one expedient after another was adopted, none of which proved satisfactory. In the meantime the girl was a danger to herself and to others she might come into contact with.

The need for some form of 'closed unit' provision to deal with this minority of cases is well known; at the moment there seems little chance of a significant amount of such provision being made available in the near future. Individual local authorities, whose responsibility such provision would be, do not have enough of these children to make the undertaking of such a difficult job seem necessary or worth while, when they are faced with so many other problems. The Regional Planning Committees, even when they see the need and would wish to fill the gap in provision, cannot undertake the task themselves. They would have to persuade one or other of the local authorities in their area to do the job. The difficulties of finding the staff and the resources to run such provision are formidable, and in the meantime the tackling of the problem goes by default.

Various local authorities and the courts have to try to deal with a number of children for whom there seems to be no treatment resource at all. It is a sad and unedifying state of affairs, which should not be tolerated by any society which wishes to think of itself as civilised.

Many such children have to return to their own homes, willy-nilly. The social workers attempt to cope with them under the provision of the care order; their task, on occasion, is almost impossible, and for some of them, it is heart-breaking. The damage caused in the lives of the rest of the family and the local community is also something to be taken into account, as well as the further damage occasioned to the children themselves.

Many of these disturbed children, usually persistent absconders already, run away to escape the supervision of the social worker. Many of them leave their own home areas, and move to the nearest large conurbation, where they can hide more easily. London has its share of these children and young people, drifting around, aimlessly, concerned to survive somehow and to escape the attention of the social services and the police, unable to cope with their own problems and not able to seek skilled help or advice of any kind for fear of being returned to the places and supervision from which they have fled. Every large city now has its contingent of such youngsters, who have moved in from outside and wish to remain hidden from all authority.

Some are helped by various voluntary organisations, and other bodies of one sort or another, who work in great difficulties, because, to a degree, they have to enter into complicity with the youngsters they seek to help, who wish to avoid all official attention. Other youngsters join into any loosely organised group that happens to be in existence—squatters groups or others, which gather together in any urban area. Some few work through their problems—many more get into even more serious trouble.

Because they are unable to obtain employment cards, they are subject to exploitation. A number of them live by casual prostitution, both boys and girls. Some of them, ironically, have run away because of emotional and sexual problems; in most cases they find themselves in a milieu which compounds those problems. A number of them have not been able to face the fact that they are, or might be, homosexual, in their own home community in which they are known; so they escape to the anonymity of the city. A number of them then become homosexual prostitutes, because it is the easiest way they know to earn a living.

Many of them have drink problems, which are rapidly increasing among teenagers. Others face drug problems, though their numbers now seem to be declining. Whatever their original problems, the sort of life they must now lead makes them far worse.

For many of them the only way to survive is through activities which infringe the law; the rolling of drunks, or would-be clients for sexual favours, petty theft, shop-lifting, the snatching of handbags, and some mugging—these are all ways by which some of them survive.

This small, floating population is difficult to reach and difficult to help; attempts to trace such youngsters, once they have run away, are not conspicuously successful. Usually they finally return home through boredom, tired of the aimless, promiscuous and uncertain life they are forced to live. Some of them manage to form relationships which tide them over for a while. Many of them come to the notice of the police once more.

The various social agencies, largely informal and voluntary, do a heroic job trying to help in every way they can. Many of them maintain a place to which these youngsters can go for help or advice; the staff try to make themselves readily available and to make and maintain contact with them in order to befriend them. It is not always easy.

Some of the local authorities try to help with grants, but often the local authority responsible for most of the youngsters is many miles away, and probably knows nothing of them, except that they have disappeared.

It is a disturbing aspect of the failure of provision. Many of the youngsters with whom I have spoken are unhappy; they feel exploited and ashamed, despite the air of bravado with which many try to hide their uneasiness on first meeting. Apart from the voluntary work of a small and dedicated band of people, there is little positive help offered to them, and on any more formal basis, they probably would not willingly accept it. Many authorities prefer to ignore the problem and try to pretend it does not exist. Yet in the large majority of cases, some local authority is responsible, because of a Care Order made by a local court.

This group presents a challenge to our concern for which we have not yet framed any fitting response—there is little doubt that one must be found, not only because of the potential damage that they represent to society, but because of the real damage which they cause in themselves.

They are the extreme edge of a band of rootless and affectionless youngsters who are a problem in every town and city. Many of them have been through the courts, and had contact with the Social Services Departments. Such provision as has been made has markedly failed to work in trying to deal with their particular problems.

They are the tip of an iceberg of unhappy, damaged and desperate youngsters, liable to create further damage and unhappiness in the lives of others as well as themselves. Many authorities prefer, as I have said, to ignore their existence, or pretend that they are not significant. I believe they represent an extreme of the children in distress, whose needs have not been met, because we have not thought through the problems and lack the will and the skill to make the resources available to help them.

Many of them end up in prison or mental hospitals; some die. Their lives are a waste we cannot afford, and their existence is a reproach to our whole society.

Damaged Children

How do we define a 'damaged' child or youth, and how do they
become so? When youngsters come to the attention of the police
and the courts, the damage is already likely to be serious, and,
in many cases, partially irremediable.

The lives of most children who can be described as damaged
are a chronicle of failure—as much in others as in themselves.
Their home and parents have failed; the local community has
failed; society has failed. A great deal of work to prevent failure
in these different areas is necessary if we are not to see the number
and forms of failure increase.

The quality of life in our community is diminished in the
diminished life of each of these children. We are still too compla-
cent about the facts of this failure, pushing them to one side by
referring to them as part of the facts of life or the real situation.
By this semantic sleight we excuse our lack of readiness to look
at the problem clearly and undertake the necessary preventive
work.

There are many words, few deeds; the essential decisions are not
those centred around individuals, but political, affecting our
whole society and its moral attitudes.

Statistically the number of children is small; so is the number
of those who contract cancer. We choose at the moment to remain remarkably insensitive to the damage done to these children;
we are extremely sensitive to the damage they do to others. That
balance of concern has to be adjusted.

By the time we deploy such resources as we command, from
the social services and other agencies, the damage has already
become well developed and cut deep. Even if a measure of success
is achieved in such remedial efforts, the damage is lasting, and an
individual life is stunted.

Chronologically the first failure usually occurs in the home.
Deprivation manifests itself very frequently in the early lives of
those most grossly disturbed and presenting the most serious

problems in later life. Seldom is there a purposeful, loving relationship within the family—here I do not count sentimentality, of which, often, a surfeit exists. For a number of children there is in no real sense a functioning home at all.

This serves to emphasise the deep-rooted nature of the problem; inadequate parents are often the victims of similar childhood experiences, and their inability to provide a meaningful home and family relationship stems from their own affectionless childhood. Their blighted lives, productive of an inability to love, blight the lives of their children. In this sense, there truly is a cycle of deprivation.

Many of these families will live in areas which are also deprived. The local community will be lacking in indigenous resources and leaders; those who administer the area, staff the schools and work in the Social Services will exercise their economic and social power and choose not to live in the area. No matter how much empathy they can command, they are essentially alien to the life style of the area they seek to help.

The horizons of such a community will be limited and real expectation modest; the prospect will be as mean as the streets, and the future as overwhelming and impersonal as the tower blocks which dominate them. The minor inadequacies and the major faults will reflect each other, until the final compound of failure is destructive to the most vulnerable and corrosive of the quality of life of all the rest.

The schools, which, in the nineteenth century were seen as beacons of progress, have become the proving grounds of failure for a significant number of children in such communities. Learning is not easy when the child comes from a background of multiple failure. For these children school is the place where failure is demonstrated and proved upon them.

They come to school with little familiarity with reading material, and vocabularies as limited as their lives; they cannot readily trust adults, because of the early failure in relationships with the adults naturally most close to them. They are not prepared to trust, because trust opens the door to rejection.

Many teachers learn to recognise these children quickly; they can identify them and their problems, but are baffled by the lack of facilities to make good the defects whose effects they are aware of. Most teachers identify their potential problem children very early in their school lives: some schools, within their limits, try to help in whatever ways they can. Very often the resources are not available in sufficient quantity and the children are too numerous.

This is true of children ascertained educationally subnormal or maladjusted, categories which have received statutory recognition and for whom remedial help should be available. For children whose initial problems are not statutorily defined—who have to move into one or other of these categories to become recipients of such help as is available!—there is less chance of help at this stage. The problems have to become worse before there is much chance of help.

Most of these children manage somehow in the infants' school. Where the system is open and flexible, activity-centred, and there is the excitement of new experience and discovery, the world seems opening to them, and most of them respond. The first signs of real trouble usually begin to appear in the junior school, where assessing children begins, and become more pronounced in the secondary school, when the first and perhaps most vital judgement has been given.

✕ Our initiation of young adults is far crueller and more élitist than almost any other society; we begin the process much earlier and prolong it much later than any other society on earth at any time in history. Education is our instrument; we are ruthless in our trial and pitiless in our rejection. ✕

These are not the avowed aims of teachers nor the goals of education; they are the effect upon those whom the whole process fails, the damaged children. Many teachers are baffled by them. They show no specific signs of maladjustment or mental inadequacy; they are marked only by their incapacity to make progress in acquiring the basic skills.

Devoted teachers will try one technique after another in an effort to achieve some progress; others will assume that the child is lazy or stubbornly recalcitrant. The needs of the child, though the teacher may or may not recognise it, are primarily social not educational.

They need reinforcement of their confidence and self-esteem. The child, lacking confidence, and subject to further loss of esteem because of failure in school, will find means to reinforce his self-image in ways which are not conducive to healthy development— usually either by withdrawal or by disruption.

The child who has missed out on basic skills will seek to reject school, before school rejects him, or her. The inability to learn will be dramatised into a refusal to learn, which, in some measure, is status-giving. If the failure is masked by confrontation, it is less demeaning, and a number of children choose this course.

It is more satisfying to the self-esteem of a teenager to provoke teachers to displays of disapproval and rejection than to admit the inability to master one or other of the basic skills. For others, perhaps less extrovert, and perhaps even more lacking in confidence, the simple way out of the problem is truancy. Through aggression or withdrawal, fight or flight, the pattern is developed. X The child who is disruptive, or the child who seeks to withdraw, both add finally to the numbers of truants. Truancy is a growing problem in inner urban communities, almost reaching epidemic proportions at some times of the year in certain schools. Some observers claim that this is happening because the processes of education have become irrelevant to certain children, lack significance, and even actively repel them. This may be part of the explanation in some cases; the question remains, how much is this a cover-story for the deep-seated lack of confidence and self-esteem operative in numbers of these children.

The school has its own categories of excellence, its own standards of achievement, and its particular marks of esteem. Consciously or unconsciously the listings are drawn up; the child at the bottom of the list suffers another loss of esteem and further damage to self-esteem.

The ordinary, reasonably well-adjusted child, with the resources of a reasonably loving and functioning home behind him, or her, can cope with mistakes and occasional failures; the damaged child has no such resource to fall back on, so that the injury is more painful. To preserve such self-esteem as survives, the child needs to demonstrate the irrelevancy of the school process. It is essential for this to be established for survival.

Many of these youngsters aspire to adulthood prematurely, telescoping the period of exploratory play and discovery that is the lot of the more fortunate child. There is no room for experiment where failure means a further devastating injury to self-esteem. These damaged children desire desperately to be grown-up, and cannot sustain the infantile part of their personality; in the confused period of emergent adulthood this makes them particularly vulnerable and much more likely to be thrown off-balance.

All children experience some form of turbulence in these formative years; the ordinary child has certain guides and controls to keep some sense of direction and location. The damaged child lacks these, and is more likely to thrust himself into adverse situations and be thrown into further confusion and off-course.

In aspiring to pseudo-adulthood, admission of inability to read is to admit to consciousness some part of the infantile experience which is the area of greatest uncertainty in the personality. 'Not doing well' at school is to be classed 'amongst the kids' when the child is wanting to be recognised as an adult.

The failure must not be admitted. All attempts to help mitigate the failure will be regarded with suspicion and must be rejected, sometimes with violence and abuse. The spiral becomes tighter and more vicious, until the only way out is a complete rebuttal of all reasonable standards and a deliberate attitude of confrontation.

All children pass through rebelliousness; it is a way of defining the emergent adult personality—in the damaged child such rebellion ceases to be creative and purposeful: it is destructive, negative and life-denying.

At present, spasmodically, and as a result of isolated individual initiatives, many schools try to cope with these children in varying ways and with varying degrees of success. The Education Welfare Officers, one of whose prime tasks the helping of such children should be, try to do what they can, but they are uncertain in part of their own role and function, and cannot command the resources, even when they see the need, to do anything truly effective. It is necessary to recognise much more clearly the particular mixture of problems we are faced with, and to concert much more systematic programmes in our efforts to help.

This will call upon the resources of departments outside the Education Department; the need for closer integration of all the resources which can be brought to bear upon such children and their families is urgent. Many people proclaim the need; there are few thoroughgoing attempts, as yet, to meet it.

We come once more to the problem of communication between the various services—specifically at this juncture between the Social Services Departments and the Education Departments. Penetration of the imperial boundaries between the two services is not always easy in either direction; Education Welfare Officers complain that the social workers do not co-operate with them, and social workers make the same complaints in reverse.

There are difficulties; some teachers do not welcome social workers into the school, because they fear that this would not be welcome to the child or the child's parents. Some social workers also feel that this is undesirable. The child may feel picked out or picked upon, and suspect that teachers or fellow-pupils are made aware of problems which he (or she) would prefer to remain concealed.

It is a difficult and delicate exercise and yet the schools and the social services need to share their knowledge and insights and concert their approaches if the damage is to be checked and possibly made good. They are concerned with the child in his whole life, and the home and school are vital parts of the child's life-experience, and any work attempted in either area should be co-ordinated.

Some teachers are suspicious of social workers, not understanding their role. They suspect social workers connive at truancy and encourage some children in their absences. Some social workers, for their part, accept the child's view of the irrelevancy of school too easily, at times, and, in their attempt to identify with the child, seem to ally themselves with the child against the teacher. This sort of misunderstanding should not be allowed to continue, but the legends on both sides continue to grow to bolster it; the losers are the children.

In cases where the home failure is compounding failure at school, the obvious need for concerted programmes of help demands the closest co-operation and understanding of all the agencies concerned; professional ethics demand this should be as comprehensive and far-reaching as possible. It is false professionalism to stand aloof on grounds of uncertainty of function and role—the need is real and the programme to meet that need must be concerted around the child, the home, the school and not around professional considerations. The problems interpenetrate the life-experience of the child, and the solutions must be interpenetrative to match.

Truancy, as anyone who has sat in a Juvenile Court will know, is always a danger signal. It is the flashing red beacon indicating that something is amiss, or soon likely to be amiss in the life of a child. The cause is not usually single or simple. When it involves a complex of problems, of which truancy is only the presenting problem, the approach must be multiple.

In attempts to help truants, many organisations have tried to develop group-schemes, free-schools and a variety of other solutions. This approach may help certain individual children, but it leaves to one side the serious failure of the school. Such organisations must always be regarded as stop-gap organisations, of uncertain life and varying effectiveness; the real solution must lie in the schools, but the schools could learn from what these groups attempt.

What is it in the school experience which enables some young-sters to assert, with some measure of truth, that the school is irrelevant to their lives? I have indicated that very often, when talking to some of these youngsters, this assertion—of irrelevancy or boredom—is advanced as a cover for a critical lack of self-esteem and lack of confidence in achievement. Nevertheless, there is some truth in it in the case of a minority of these children. This attitude has received reinforcement from the lengthening of the period of compulsory school, which has hit a number of children who had counted on leaving school on one date, and find their day of escape postponed. It is the fact that leaving school is seen as the day of escape which is important.

Inevitably, with this group, we will work through the situation. Children beginning school now will know how long they will have to remain. It still is a fact that for a number of children the school, and the idea of school, has failed.

It has, I believe, something to do with what I have described as 'pseudo-adulthood'. The belief that release from school opens a new era of freedom. It seems to be a fact that two groups of people, intellectually poles apart, have one strand of personality in common; both the pseudo-adult, with aspirations to premature maturity, and the perpetual student, with a desire to play out a role that is neither adult nor responsible, seem to lack the capacity to subsume part of their infantile experience into their personality.

It is a sad fact that many of the children who escape from school into pseudo-adulthood are ill-equipped to take on the responsi-bilities of adult life, with the necessary making of judgements and organisational forethought that this entails. The chief difference between the perpetual student and the pseudo-adult is one of social background; the perpetual student commands the resources to perpetuate his or her adolescence, particularly adolescent rebellion, into later life—the youngster snatching at premature adulthood does not command these resources, but also has to adopt the posture of rebellion, for reasons I have already outlined.

It is the second category which is more likely to come into conflict with the law: the most the former category can do is come in conflict, most of the time, with the administrators of further education.

In both cases there is a failure to integrate the whole life-experience at that time into the adult personality. The damaged child cannot have such integrity because of the fundamental loss of self-esteem, which means continual attention-seeking, often through rebellion. Being known as the trouble-maker is as much attention-seeking, for the larger part of the time, as is the continual childishness of the more obvious attention-seeker, on the other side of the behavioural coin.

The children we are concerned with have 'come to the attention of the police', of the social services, or the court. Lack of attention early in life has forced them into a stance of provocation; they, who have been ignored, more or less proclaim, 'You will notice me.' Unfortunately they come to notice too late.

The chief failure of the modern school lies in the fact that educationists have still failed to resolve the dilemma which has faced them over the centuries—the transition from child to adolescent to adult. With all children remaining at school for a longer time, this failure has been accentuated in the case of the children who are not motivated to continue studying.

Various schemes of education now see the role of the school as dynamic and developing; in practice, for many youngsters it seems to be more of the same thing for a longer time. Imparting knowledge and stimulating enquiry and curiosity have not gone hand in hand. In the situation prevailing in many of the areas of our towns and cities, with large classes and lack of staff, it is almost impossible. The will is not lacking amongst most teachers —again it is a lack of resources.

There is a much more sensitive boundary than that between two departments of the local authority or two social agencies; it is the frontier between the two societies within our country, and we send children through the minefields to discover the division for themselves.

The child who is already damaged by home experience is peculiarly sensitive to, even if not conscious of, these divisions, and is least able to cope with them. The more able child learns a degree of conformity as part of his protective colouring (whether this is desirable or not); the less able child, less able to adapt, blunders on into new disasters (even though they may seem, initially, minor failures to the outsider).

The child, in theory, is learning the intellectual and social values of society—for the children we are concerned with, these values are of an alien society. We pay a degree of attention to the problem of immigrants within our community, but have little consciousness still of the children who cross the frontier into an alien world when they enter school. Yet for many children this is the case, and it remains so, even when we choose to ignore it.

In this alien world the child needs approval, as do all children, but the need of the damaged child is that much greater and much less likely to be won, except from the teacher of particularly wide understanding, who is probably overwhelmed by the task in the moment of the realisation of need.

School is supposed to deepen and widen the child's outlook and experience; at the same time it multiplies the opportunities for failure. Each failure will mean a loss of esteem, and, most damagingly, self-esteem; the approval of adults, the good opinion of other children cannot be won in accepted ways—there is a need, if the child is not to be crushed, to win esteem in other ways, less approved of, and more likely to create trouble and produce conflict.

The edge between the wider standards of society, embodied in the school, and the standards of the smaller sub-grouping (sometimes of one or of a small group) rubs raw and inflames the conflict. The sore spot creates an intense awareness of both sets of standards—and defiance of those standards still admits of their possible worthiness.

In adolescence the youngster needs to discover some focus of identity and relate the newly emergent identity with the standards by which he, or she, has already failed. His own standards are relatively independent of the values of adults around him; he is a failure in the terms of the values of those adults. Yet in working through to the discovery of an adult personality he will have created an ideal self, and he judges his real self against the ideal and also against the standards of adults—the echoes and reflections from one self to the other create an almost hallucinatory chaos. Few adults would not become disorientated, subject to such challenging uncertainties and pressures, despite their greater experience and more assured sense of identity; for these youngsters the situation is one of increasing bewilderment and confusion.

The fact that many of these youngsters can settle back into a reasonably stable life after the turbulent years of adolescence demonstrates the particular crisis of the school years and adolescence. Once free from school they can move into groups whose judgements are more akin to their own, where they are no longer so pointedly subject to the scrutiny of an alien community. The school child has no such refuge, except through rejection of the school, truancy and possible delinquency.

Most children want to do well; deliberate refusal of approval is rare. Like most of us they want to be liked, appreciated and admired. But the child who has failed in relationships within the home will fail most likely also in the school. The failure in school will increase the likelihood of further failure in social relations with other adults.

It is thus no mystery that the peak years for conflict with the law should be the last years of school and the first few after leaving school. We have now so ordered things that this is almost inevitable. We have built turbulence into the system so that it whirls youngsters into conflict and confrontation. The means we deploy, at the moment, to contain this situation and try to remedy it are inadequate, clumsy and too late.

It is easier to concern ourselves with particular children, and to see their bad behaviour as of their own making. It is much more difficult to determine the general conditions which can manufacture the circumstances which can produce such children and try to discover ways to help them. The courts, the social workers, the police are dealing with individual symptoms, while all of them are uneasily aware of the general malaise which none of them can reach far into nor help much to deal with.

It is a perennial cry; it is a disturbing attitude for some people, because they choose not to want to know. It is a product of poverty; not only in financial and economic terms—in some measure, at least, these have been dealt with, though not satisfactorily—but poverty of life, poverty of imagination (particularly on the part of the authorities), poverty of opportunity and poverty of resources to deal with the situation.

While possibly accepting this picture of the background of many such children it is important not to lose the individual case in generalities; the child or young person must never become a case or a symptom. This is finally to deny the identity of the emergent adult, and to complete the work of alienation. All social agencies face this crux; the maintenance of the individual in the morass of conflicting pressures and overwhelming complexities of the modern condition, especially in the inner urban area.

The human scale has gone from much of life already in areas of our cities and towns; in seeking to cope with the larger problem we must not lose sight of the individual suffering of the girl or boy, nor allow our sensitivity to be overwhelmed by the size of the fundamental problems.

Those who argue that these matters are the unchanging facts of life and those who see the general problem as so complex as to be insoluble join hands in the gentle keening of despair. We need something more than this if we are not to connive at the destruction of more youngsters and the diminishing of our lives as a community.

We should make the home, the school and the community central to the child's experience; for too many of these children it is the court which has become the central factor. In the limited context of the court it is easier, on occasion, to comprehend the problem, but the court can do little to help the child cope. It is one more area of sensitization which needs to be enlarged; good magistrates are properly sensitized to the point where they recognise the limitations of what they can do.

10

Intermediate Treatment

Ironically, there is one last treatment to hand, which might, in fact, bring about the essential, coherent assault on the factors which do damage to the child or young person.

It is little in itself, but it embodies the germ of something which might grow in ways which would make good many of the present deficiences. I am referring to the provision in Section 12 of the Children & Young Persons Act which has been given the bastard name of Intermediate Treatment. This statement will provoke derision from many professional workers, but I believe it to be true.

I have already referred to the powers given under the Children & Young Persons Act of 1963, to local government departments to do preventive work; this power was never used to mount the bold and basic attack on deprivation in all its manifestations, familial and communal, that had been hoped for. This was due partly to lack of finance, partly lack of human resources, and partly lack of nerve and will. Under the provision of Intermediate Treatment, if it is used and developed with imagination, courage and skill, the opportunity returns by the back door.

Intermediate Treatment derives from the power given to the court to attach certain conditions to Supervision Orders. This power was available to the court when making Probation Orders and the earlier form of Supervision Order, before that was superseded. Under the earlier dispensation, however, the emphasis was on containment and restriction, rather than on positive, remedial treatment.

Previously court orders had distinguished critically between those which entailed removal from home and those which sought to work with the child or young person within the community. The description, Intermediate Treatment, derives from that distinction, even though, in fact, it no longer exists in the orders that the court can make. It is seen as intermediate between the two courses of action—removal from home or remaining at home under supervision.

Intermediate Treatment is intended to bring the child or youth into contact with new environments, both physical and mental, new situations and new opportunities, while working with him in the community that he knows best. Most important of all, it is not intended that the process should be punitive; it is essentially remedial and preventative.

It may incorporate a period away from home, in the form of residential courses, for a limited period, or it may establish participation in non-residential activity of many different kinds within the home community, or a combination of the two—all these to be deployed in conjunction with the supportive treatment of the Supervision Order.

The time spent away from home is limited; the subject of the order can be instructed to live at a specified place for a period not exceeding ninety days, beginning with the first year of the order. The length of time (as a maximum) spent away from home will be set by the court within the statutory maximum; the officer appointed by the court as supervisor, either a probation officer or social worker, will be responsible for planning the course, the timing and the overall structure of treatment.

The obvious virtue in this approach is its flexibility and capacity for response to need. If there is a situation in the home or school which has become impossible for the youngster, the parents, the school, or all of them, removal can provide a breathing space; at the same time work with the youngster and with the home can prepare both for the time when he returns home.

The negative aspect of removal from an immediate crisis is important, but the opportunity to use the time constructively means special planning and forethought. Placement might be in any one of a number of establishments which may be able to offer something of value to a youngster at a given time and over a limited period; it could be in a hostel, a community home, a voluntary home, on a course, or in any other form of residential provision which meets the needs of the youngster at that particular moment.

The second alternative would involve temporary removal from home for a period or periods totalling not more than thirty days in each year for which the order is effective. The use of this time is left very flexible indeed; it might include time away from home over weekends, for a week, or for a series of weekends, coupled with attendance at some form of organised activity within the community, on specified evenings or for whole days.

This is the framework; it is as flexible as possible, consonant with safeguarding the rights of the child.

When social workers ask what is Intermediate Treatment and I reply, 'what you care to make it,' I think that is the truth of the situation. Because it is so flexible it can be responsive to the needs of the subject as they change and modify in ways which no other form of treatment can match.

It is intended that the plan should be more structured than the ordinary Supervision Order, and the making of the order places upon the responsible local government agency the duty to spend such money as is required to carry through the programme of treatment once it has been devised. This is important. It has made local authorities realise that they have a financial duty in respect of this order which is statutory. This awareness has served to focus attention on similar expenditure, used by way of prevention, which might bring about intervention earlier in the life of the child, and save more expensive provision later, when the child is more damaged and has attracted the attention of the court.

More important than this aspect, however, is the impulse towards co-operation between the various agencies which Intermediate Treatment will generate. The supervising officer will require the help of agencies outside his own service to make the treatment effective.

Intermediate Treatment may well prove to be the catalyst in this situation, where many agencies, with different disciplines, have long been concerned with children yet have significantly failed to co-operate and communicate freely and effectively. The necessary channels of communication, once opened, may carry many surprising messages, and extend co-operation from one very narrow and limited aspect of their various functions, across the whole field of their mutual concern. Nothing would bring greater benefit to all children in need than this development, if it were to come about.

The court will make an Intermediate Treatment order on the recommendation of the Social Services Department or the Probation Service. The supervising officer will need to know the child thoroughly if an effective system of treatment is to be devised.

The essential step will be the discovery of some 'interest hook' on which to hang the treatment. If this proves difficult, then the ability to remove the child from home for a short period at the beginning of treatment is all important.

Intermediate Treatment is based on the belief, expressed by Sir Keith Joseph, when Secretary of State for the Department of Health and Social Services, that the need is to make the child feel involved once more in the community.

The wider the opportunities and satisfactions which our society offers its members, the more acute are the problems of adjustment which it poses to a minority of young people. The factors which may lead to a child growing up feeling 'out of it all' are many. So are the ways in which the child's predicament can come to our notice—through truancy or non-achievement at school, through family casework by one of the statutory or voluntary agencies for social service, or (all too often) through a first appearance before the courts.

Plainly we need new ways in which we can help such young people to overcome their difficulties.

Intermediate Treatment provides the court with a new option in their choice of ways of trying to solve the problems. It also offers a series of options to the supervising officer. It is a last try, before removal to an institution, at fitting the child back into the community.

It is all the more important when we realise that most of the young people who come into conflict with the law during adolescence do not progress into a life of crime. If they do continue to run foul of the law, they become inadequate offenders, not the dramatic villains of the crimes which make newspaper headlines.

It must be faced that we do not know the specific reasons why they come into attitudes of conflict in the first place, nor do we know why, at some age between nineteen and twenty-three, they stop, for the most part. A device which extends the possibility of holding them in the community, rather than expelling them into some form of institution, and which at the same time tries to develop services which can diminish the conflict or remove it completely is of importance.

It is important, too, in that it can be 'personalised' in ways which most other forms of treatment cannot match—because of its flexibility. If it is to succeed, however, it must be used imaginatively and directed to specific individual needs, and the early study of the subject of the order must be as thorough and sensitive as possible. Intermediate Treatment must never become just another expedient when no one has any further ideas about what to do.

Indeed, properly, the study should be made before an Intermediate Treatment Order is recommended to the court. The fuller the information accompanying the recommendation for Intermediate Treatment, the better the prospect for the treatment if the court makes such an order.

The ultimate planning of Intermediate Treatment is in the hands of the Regional Planning Committees; they will spread the umbrella under which the scheme works. The immediate planning is the responsibility of the individual social worker, faced with a particular subject.

The discovery of what I have called an 'interest hook' is the first step; it implies working closely with the youngster to discover some activity which he finds relevant and which will generate enthusiasm—for this may be used as a possible structure of treatment.

What are 'interest hooks'?

They are the areas in a youngster's developing interests which might be used in the course of the treatment to involve him in activities and relationships which help him to 'socialise' in ways which will make his conflicting behaviour less likely to recur. Hopefully they will enhance his life experience at the same time.

The ultimate test of success of such an order would be if the youngster continued in the activities to which he or she had been introduced once the compulsion of the order was removed. Such experiences should offer new perspectives to him, and at the same time open up new opportunities of self-realisation or fulfilment, coupled with some sense of achievement. The two desirable ends would be to bring him into meaningful and worthwhile relations with some people of the same age, and some adults, and to begin to widen his outlook so that he could comprehend activities other than delinquent or deviant ones. I do not believe it is possible to achieve the one without the other.

In short, it is an attempt to make good some of the damage that has happened earlier in life. The improvement of the self-image, the arousal of expectation and the generating of new energies, directed to worthwhile ends. Any statement of this sort begs many questions, as I am all too well aware, but these would seem to be desirable objects, however they are interpreted, and whatever the values by which they are judged.

There would seem to be broadly two types of youngster for whom Intermediate Treatment would be most suitable; those whose energies are not properly contained or used in their every-day lives at the moment, and those others, more given to withdrawal from life, who need to be stimulated to more activity and to be brought into the life of their contemporaries. In a sense these two types are mirror-images of one another; they are alike in their lack of achievement and their poor self-image.

It is obvious that there will be as many problems as children or young persons; the need will always be to discover, so far as it is possible, what sorts of problems face an individual child, and to try to deal with those as sensitively and as imaginatively as possible.

Each scheme must have an Intermediate Treatment officer—someone whose fulltime job it is to organise and co-ordinate the flow of information about all available resources and possible approaches. Any social worker charged with the supervision of a child under an Intermediate Treatment Order will then have one person to turn to for help, guidance and information. The officer will have a number of essential jobs to do, amongst which are the following:

1. To be available, especially to the other officers in the department.

2. To ensure that all available information is gathered in, processed, properly codified, interpreted and kept up-to-date.

3. To maintain a lively contact with the local court, and to ensure a proper two-way flow of information between the magistrates and other officers of the court and the Social Services Department.

4. To ensure that contacts between the schools, the youth services and the police are of the kind that can enhance the prospects of success for those subject to Intermediate Treatment.

5. To make contact with all other agencies which may be of help developing Intermediate Treatment schemes; this will entail a thorough knowledge of all the voluntary and statutory agencies in the area, of use in such treatment. It is important that these contacts be as vivid and direct as possible—for they and the information they provide will be invaluable to the individual worker supervising a case.

6. To undertake as much work as possible in the general community. The generation of good will and understanding there, by keeping them informed and winning as much involvement and co-operation from them as possible, might develop new resources and new methods of working.

7. To compile a list of all relevant activities in the community of an organised or structured sort which might be of use in Intermediate Treatment: this would include not only boys' clubs, youth clubs, scouts, and the more obvious activities, but also dramatic societies, folk clubs, car and motor-cycle clubs, animal breeding clubs, dog clubs, pigeon clubs, art groups, music societies and all the many and varied activities and pursuits which people organise themselves to participate in, study or follow. The more comprehensive this list, the more likely it may be that the supervising officer will be able to find a friendly group or adult who will help him with a particular boy or girl.

This is very important, because the more community involvement there is in a scheme which depends upon treating the child's problems within the community, the better. Of course we are immediately in the presence of a particular professional complex of problems; the willingness, or otherwise, to co-operate with members of the public in situations which are part of a professional scheme of treatment when the members of the public are not professionally trained in social service skills.

No one should minimise the problems in this area—winning co-operation between the club worker and the trained youth worker and the social worker is difficult enough at times. To suggest that some part of the treatment might depend upon the intelligent co-operation of members of the public is inviting trouble in the eyes of many social workers. But it is an important opportunity which should be considered carefully, and certainly not ignored. It could prove very fruitful indeed. Too often social workers complain of the lack of interest on the part of the general public in their work; they ascribe some part of their low status and low pay to this indifference, and some complain of the sense of working in a vacuum because of the public's lack of understanding of their role.

Intermediate Treatment, fully understood and properly organised, could provide a bridge not only between different professional disciplines, but also to the general public. There are people of good will (not busy-bodies or bourgeois do-gooders exclusively!) whose particular life experience would enable them to make contact with youngsters in ways not possible for the social worker.

This has been shown in various organisations already, where ex-drug addicts have been most successful in helping present addicts, and ex-alcoholics have given support to those still engaged in the battle with alcohol, where ex-prisoners and ex-Borstal inmates have been strikingly successful in enabling newly released prisoners to adjust to society more smoothly on release.

It is this same pool of experience and particular set of insights which Intermediate Treatment could tap for a number of those needing help; older men and women, who have themselves experienced the same, or similar, problems in their lives, who would be only too willing to extend similar help to youngsters in the throes of the turbulence of adolescence.

Such working together would create new perspectives for young people in trouble and would help to educate the general public in what is being attempted. If Intermediate Treatment is to succeed it must involve the community in what is a community problem. Social workers should not flinch from this; their professional status is now sufficiently sure for them to be able to enlist and use such aid without fear of 'diluting' their own profession or jeopardising their own skills, and they should never fear the intrusion of people from outside willing to work with them and accept their professional guidance.

There will, of course, be difficulties, but they should not prove insuperable. Indeed, such working together might provide both support and refreshment to many social workers—something which all those working in Social Services Departments should be alive to.

The particular value of Intermediate Treatment is that it can bring social workers into practical working relations with professionally trained people from other disciplines and with the general public to the mutual advantage of both, leading to an increase in the exchange of ideas and to the growth of insight and understanding.

As the tendency to treat more and more people in the community develops, this experience will be of particular value. It so happens that Intermediate Treatment is one way of stimulating and canalising this exchange, which could provide valuable lessons for future development. It would bring the social worker into relationships with the general public where their contact is not with 'client' figures, but ordinary people with their own independent point of view, attitudes and prejudices. It should prove an interesting and salutary experience for all concerned.

Although everyone will complain of pressure of work, lack of time or energy, it is often surprising how new energy, new enthusiasm and new capacities can be summoned up when people are faced with a particular young person in a situation where they can help. This form of reinforcement should be welcome to social workers, unless their insecurity in their own role has gone farther than I have yet experienced.

There would never be any doubt about who was controlling the situation; the law specifically lays the duty on the supervising officer and the court would specify that. The whole process, in each case, would be completely under the control of the social worker and the department. But if a worthwhile relationship could be created between a youngster and some other individual, under the umbrella of Intermediate Treatment, a major step towards success would have been taken. And if social workers feel they can collaborate with the public, the treatment can enjoy a new dimension of flexibility in approach.

Bringing together a particular group or individual and the subject of an order is always possible under any Intermediate Treatment scheme; there will be organisations, clubs, groups and other associations nominated under the scheme—the adult who might be able to help a particular youngster can join one or other of these organisations as an ancillary helper, and the first step is achieved. The more imaginatively the list of organisations is broadened, the less is the necessity for devices of this sort.

Organisations which are purposefully structured and which can offer some potential in this field should be encouraged to register; there is no compulsion upon them to accept any particular youngster. By registering all they do is to announce their willingness to help if the right subject comes along—theirs would always be the choice, when asked to help a particular youngster, and they can say nay as easily as yea. It might very well be that there is no point in turning to them for a considerable time, but it would always be useful for the Intermediate Treatment officer to know that the facilities of any given organisation were available and might be turned to if the occasion arose; it might also suggest different and more interesting approaches to schemes of treatment for those charged with this task.

A situation which arose in my own experience, before there was the possibility of Intermediate Treatment as such, illustrates how important flexibility is, and how one should be ready to include unforeseen opportunities in the treatment.

A particular child, not in the context of a court, had begun to draw attention to himself through bullying, a degree of irrational behaviour and marked aggression both towards other youngsters and the weaker members of staff. He was a child who came to notice in a mass of children with problems. In the course of talking to him about his behaviour, because it had been suggested to me that quite serious measures to control him would have to be taken (and I would have been required to give my consent to these steps), it emerged, quite unexpectedly, that he was interested in engraving. Nothing more unlikely as an interest for this particular youngster could have been suggested if the reports of those who had had to deal with him had been studied in isolation.

It emerged that he had kept this interest secret because he was a little ashamed of it—it did not consort with the tough image he was busy creating around himself, and into which he was anxious to retreat. Even when I was told the secret, I was sworn to keep it between us.

It did seem a possible 'interest hook'. I made some enquiries and found that amongst my own constituents was a retired printer, whose hobby was engraving. He and the boy were brought together; a rather studious and gentle old-aged pensioner and a youngster well on the way to earning the label 'thug'. Despite every disparity between them, they had the one common enthusiasm. The boy was delighted to be able to discuss the technicalities of the process of engraving. The boy needed lodgings, since he was about to leave the residential school; the old man offered them, and his wife became the boy's landlady.

More important than that, they organised, through the old man's union connections, the admission of the boy to the print trade. It was a success (and everyone remembers the successes), but I quote it to point out how essential it is to be sensitive in exploring youngster's interests in this search for the 'interest hook' and to remind anyone who has to do so how important it is to look behind the carapace that many youngsters create to protect themselves from further hurt in the troubles that they find themselves in.

Another instance of an unlikely interest is of use in making this point. Again it was of a boy who had been involved in disruption at school and in some senseless vandalism along with a group of youngsters on a housing estate. Within a year the reports said that his character appeared to have changed: he was causing trouble at school, truanting, and taking up with a particular gang of toughs, and spending a great deal of time in cafés.

The social worker gave a very detailed report to the court, setting out his background history; and, almost in passing, there was a remark that the boy had claimed, during interview, to be interested in the theatre. When this was mentioned in court the boy shied away from the idea in some embarrassment. In my experience many youngsters claim interest in the theatre, but as a kind of daydream in which they see themselves as a famous film star. At first it seemed as if this was the case with this particular boy, that it was all part of an adolescent fantasy.

But in a closer talk with him, myself and the social worker— although it seemed improbable—it emerged that the boy was interested in the theatre in more practical terms. He had read what he could, but his knowledge of the sort of books he wanted was limited. When, with the aid of the social worker, this interest was developed a little more, he became quite absorbed and enthusiastic. When he was asked why he had never sought any help, and seemed ashamed of his interest being discussed, he became uneasy. In a subsequent discussion, when it was pointed out to him that there were two or three good local dramatic societies in his immediate neighbourhood, who did good practical work, and would have been glad of his help, he said two important things. The first was that 'My mates would think I was a poufter!' and the second that he had listened to some members of one drama society talking and thought they would think his accent funny.

Perhaps the most important point to be drawn from this story is the evidence of the conflict of images; peer pressure and peer approval were a matter of concern to this particular youngster. So was his fear of rejection by people who might think him funny in the way he spoke.

An Intermediate Treatment Order, which 'compelled' him to join in with others engaged in activities close to his hidden interest would have enabled him to become involved with people who might have helped him, while at the same time he could have pointed to the court as the people who were compelling him to undertake this work, so maintaining his good standing with that particular peer group until he no longer needed it, or was independent enough to go his own way.

So some part of the compulsion can be useful in certain circumstances: when a youngster can point to compulsion, even when the court is pushing him in the direction that, secretly, he wishes to go.

I am not suggesting that there are large numbers interested either in the arts of printing or the threatre in the community of disturbed youngsters. These two are remembered because of their rarity.

But there may be other interests unfulfilled, almost unacknowledged, in some youngsters, which their background has either precluded or made seem remote, and which might not be suspected unless a degree of sympathy and concern is brought to their problems. In both these instances the normal reports upon these boys gave no inkling of these interests, and yet they existed and were useful in helping them.

There is also the feeling amongst some young people that certain groups will not welcome them. I have already mentioned the boy and the accents of a dramatic society; this is true of other groups and activities as well.

There are numbers of people who might benefit from certain services, which others take for granted, and yet they are reluctant to turn to them—they believe, for some reason, possibly their own poor self-image, that these services or activities are not for them. They are aware of a barrier between themselves and other people—people with a different accent or outlook, described as 'posh' or some other word which emphasises the divisions in society: all those lumped together as 'Them' as opposed to the 'Us' to which they belong.

Various advertising campaigns have been developed to try to counter this feeling of diffidence. Modern banks, for instance, have spent large sums of money in showing friendly bank managers in an effort to attract the custom of 'C' and 'D' stream customers. They are aware that there are large numbers of people who do not believe that banks are for them, that they do not belong in a bank and would not be welcomed attempting to use its services. The advertising campaign is intended to break down that attitude.

Banks do not spend money lightly; they know what they want and they devise ways to achieve their ends. The same problem applies amongst the families and youngsters who are our particular interest, and we must be as alert to similar attitudes. There are youngsters who do not feel that theatrical clubs or music societies are for them, even if they would wish to attend them.

One boy, guilty of gross cruelty to some horses, had built a resentment against a particular riding school to such a pitch that he injured the animals, even though he wished to ride; he felt that the youngsters who attended the riding school, with what he called their 'cut-glass' accents, would never have accepted him, even though he had the money to pay. Maybe some of the senseless violence and vandalism reflects a degree of alienation of this kind, which Intermediate Treatment might be able to overcome, given the good will of various organisations in the community.

We are here very much concerned with the status of certain youngsters, not only with how we see them, but how they see themselves—or how they have been taught to see themselves. They believe they are excluded from certain activities; numbers of them do not believe they would be accepted in ordinary boys' clubs or youth clubs, because they are aware of the differences of background and possible accent. Many of them need a first push, given by a sympathetic adult, through the door of a youth club or into some other activity, so that they may find their way back into the mainstream of ordinary teenage activity. Where they find congenial company and some form of satisfaction at the moment is with a group of disaffected youngsters whose activities, like their own, tend towards delinquent behaviour and vandalism; acceptance in a group which is engaged in some purposive activity, once it has been accorded, can go a long way to coping with some of their frustration.

Intermediate Treatment ought to be able to do something for youngsters in this situation, and enable them to re-establish contacts with other youngsters and settle into activities which interest them and can help create a better self-image.

This is an important gain, where it is possible to achieve it. Much of the refusal to join in these activities is defensive—rather than be hurt by being snubbed they affect to despise the activities offered and the organisations which offer them. At times there are outbreaks of violence in certain clubs, part of which stems from this very kind of resentment.

As these youngsters rejected school, before school rejected them, in an effort to preserve some status amongst their peers, so they will reject clubs and other organisations. Many of them respond well when they are given a sympathetic reception and are not treated as something strange or peculiar.

The first weeks of such an association, especially where there is an element of compulsion, can, of course, be very difficult. The youngsters are on the alert for snubs, whether intentional or not, and hypersensitive; they are only too ready to march out of a situation where they are made conspicuous by their accent or their lack of '*nous*'.

This poses very real problems for club leaders and youth workers. They do not want to pick out the youngster under Intermediate Treatment by any special form of treatment; they must not seem to pay too much attention to such a youngster, for that immediately makes them conspicuous. Any request to the rest of the members to treat a particular newly joined member with special consideration could also carry dangers, and create new kinds of difficulty. The youngster wants to be accepted in his own right, not picked out as some peculiar specimen—the moment that happens the process is marked for self-defeat.

The relationship, therefore, between the supervising social worker and the club leader must be discreet. The social worker and the club leader must know the facts of the subject's background—but it would be fatal if this sort of information leaked through to the general membership of the club. One wrong word, one false attitude, would destroy everything, and the subject of the order would withdraw, probably with his earlier suspicions and resentment reinforced, and in a worse condition than before the Intermediate Treatment order was made.

The sensitivity of many youngsters, who, on the surface, assume an attitude of indifference or defiance, is quite remarkable; their pose of indifference is a cover for their fear of being hurt. Their involved acceptance can often win a ready response, but the person working with them has to be prepared to be tested. They will push hard to learn the limits of tolerance and understanding, usually after the first few contacts, and it is during this very difficult period that the greatest understanding and firmness is needed of the responsible adults. Only after this period will the youngster finally begin to settle in, feel accepted and begin to respond spontaneously to the group.

The problem with the more withdrawn type of child or young person is somewhat different. Their shyness masks the same uncertainty. For them, too much intrusion would drive them away. They need to be brought slowly into the life of the group, and not picked out in any special way, until their confidence grows and they begin to relax into a degree of acceptance.

11

The Youth Services

The reason why many different professional disciplines recoil from Intermediate Treatment stems only in part from its hybrid nature—the impure mingling of different professional activities, as some people see it. A more interesting reason lies in the fact that it calls into question, at a very basic and sensitive level, the purposes and processes of a number of these professions. Not least is this true of the Youth Services.

If treatment is to be meaningful for many youngsters, involvement in youth activities within the community, in all their variety, is an important element.

If the aim is to bring the subject of an order back into something like the mainstream of the community's life (at whatever level) one thing is necessary—the creation of valid and significant relationships with people near the youngster's age and with some adults. Most of the purposive and active organisations can be seen as possible means to this end. Any activity or group which can provide the ambience in which this might be achieved should be considered if it seems likely to meet a particular subject's needs.

Pre-eminent amongst such organisations should be the youth clubs. This means, however, a close look at what various types of club and youth organisations do at present, and what their offering to young people amounts to. Intermediate Treatment calls for youth-orientated activities—but some youth organisations have their activities centred elsewhere, in adults' preconceptions of what they believe youngsters should want, rather than in what the youngsters themselves believe they need.

Much of the ineffectiveness of many of the present youth organisations stems from this attitude—they are far too paternalistic for youngsters who are seeking to establish their own identity and ethos against that of the parent generation.

This is very often the view of social workers, who regard much youth work as irrelevant. They do not believe that it addresses itself to the realities of the situation of many of the more deprived and damaged children in the community who should be its prime concern. Intermediate Treatment would bring Social workers and youth workers into a dialogue which would benefit both. The questions the social workers might ask of the youth service are the same questions which many youth workers wish to ask of the organisations of which they are part.

Youth workers who run clubs take, broadly, two attitudes towards Intermediate Treatment—and these differing attitudes reflect differences within the movement itself. Some youth workers looking at Intermediate Treatment requirements in so far as they affect them, take the view that they have been doing this work ever since they began in the service and can see nothing new in what they are being asked to do now. At the other end of the scale are certain club leaders who want nothing to do with Intermediate Treatment at all, and argue that they would not take in anyone who did not come to them voluntarily. But behind this pure attitude lies another, which was voiced by one club leader in the following terms: 'I run a nice club, for nice kids, from nice homes, who have nice parents. I want nothing to do with delinquents, because then we would lose the nice kids.'

The fact that the youth service is passing through a crisis of identity and function complicates the picture somewhat—and again Intermediate Treatment becomes a catalyst in this situation.

The view of many youth workers and club leaders that they have been doing this sort of job for years is only partly true, and valid only to a certain point. The children who have come to them in the past have come voluntarily, and have shown some desire for involvement with the club. The children who will come to them under Intermediate Treatment come as the result of a court order; these may very often seem to be the same sort of young people, and may present problems and characteristics which, while not essentially different, will probably be more marked and may be of a more worrying degree of difficulty.

Initially there may be more reluctance on the part of the youngsters to involve themselves; there will almost certainly be a higher degree of suspicion of adults and their intentions. There will always be a testing-out period of the leader and the club, which might be critical for the development of relationships between the subject of the order, the leader and the members of the club.

The club leader, wishing to do his best for everyone concerned,

5

will have to weigh his obligation to his club and members against the needs and requirements of a particular individual referred to him by a social worker. He will, of course, have the support of the social worker, but the day-to-day working with the youngster in the context of the club will devolve upon the youth worker.

The success or failure of the order may well depend on the type of leader and the sort of club he tries to run—factors which are obviously interrelated. The matching of the youngster seeking help, the leader and the club is in itself a delicate operation and much of the success or failure will turn upon this early decision.

Intermediate Treatment has, in some measure, exposed the dichotomy of the youth services and workers, and for some this has been a painful experience. Many clubs are activity-centred, and their orientation is towards success in running team sports and mounting organised events. The leader measures his successes, and is judged by them, more than in terms of personal relationships—always something more difficult to judge, in any case. (This caricatures the position, somewhat, as nearly all generalisations do! However, there is a core of truth in this observation.)

Effective personal relationships, in this view, are a by-product of successful organisation: this is a valid point of view, and is a successful method of working with many youngsters. It is less likely to be successful, especially initially, with youngsters who might be made the subject of Intermediate Treatment Orders.

Many of the children subject to such orders will have experienced so much failure in their lives that any achievement they have ever approached has probably been in directions seen as undesirable by the adult world at large. A highly organised, competitive atmosphere is not the most useful or beneficial for them. Many cannot match the expectations of certain club leaders, and their inadequacies are the more glaringly exposed.

The ready assumption that it is possible to work with disturbed youngsters within the context of clubs organised on this basis must be challenged. It may be possible and fruitful for some; it is never likely to be very easy.

Not all clubs are of this kind, of course. Many are concerned primarily with developing relationships and individual personality through other means, with organised activities treated in a useful, but subsidiary, role. Between the one extreme and the other, the highly directed and organised club on the one hand,

and the easy-going, less structured club (or, at least, with the structure less close to the surface) lies a whole range of clubs demonstrating wide variations of emphasis.

Many clubs are meeting places for youngsters, whose activities are determined, in large measure, by the members themselves. This type of club is more likely to meet the 'socialising' need of certain youngsters more appropriately, especially in the early days of any Intermediate Treatment scheme. The difficulty with some of these clubs is the view expressed by some social workers that they are so unstructured that they might not prove acceptable to the court— in fact, the court's approval is not needed, so that objection falls by the way.

Some of the leaders of these types of clubs, are, however, uneasy themselves. They fear that the invasion of a significant number of more disturbed youngsters, who might possibly bring along members of their own 'gang', might subvert the life of the club, and undo all the work that is already being done for its ordinary members. This is always a danger, but it exists whether youngsters arrive at the club from the court or out of the ordinary community, without any brush with the law. Such clubs always have a precarious existence, in one sense, in that their membership is always changing: the good club leader learns how to remain discreetly in control of a fluid situation—it is part of his particular skill.

Even where club leaders feel that they might be able to help certain youngsters, many of them are uneasy about the reaction of their untrained 'assistants'. These are other adults, working with the youngsters, under the guidance of the leader, who might not welcome such an initiative and then withdraw from the club through disapproval or some initial difficulty. Since many clubs rely very heavily on the devoted work of such people, whose contribution and enthusiasm has been of great importance in the life of many clubs, this is a serious factor.

Discussion about the degree of effectiveness of clubs' contribution to Intermediate Treatment has highlighted a number of problems and issues which were already evident in some capacity, but which have come into focus with the introduction of Intermediate Treatment. Even such organisations as the National Association of Boys' Clubs, which made a positive effort to help, have experienced some disenchantment. This arose from a number of causes.

The initial enthusiasm of some club-leaders and workers dissipated rapidly when their first contact with social workers made it clear that the latter viewed their work with a high degree of scepticism, and, in some instances, distrust and dislike. Those who first introduced the concept of Intermediate Treatment seemed to place great importance and a degree of reliance on existing youth organisations and services. Many of the schemes submitted by Regional Planning Committees, however, did not seem to emphasise that role to quite the degree that club-leaders and youth-leaders had anticipated.

Moreover, there was considerable delay between first mention of the Treatment and its implementation; we are still without very much information of how frequently courts intend to use Intermediate Treatment, and what kinds of youngsters are being made the subject of orders.

The delay between mooting the concept and its practical implementation led to a loss of interest and enthusiasm, even amongst those who had been fired with the idea. The varying approach of different authorities makes it more difficult to produce clear guidelines on what is expected, what might be offered and what might be achieved.

As local authorities have begun to form their precise proposals for implementation, numbers of them seem to have retreated in some measure from the supposed co-operative effort with youth workers and other services. Some of the reasons have already been mentioned.

There is much talk, in some Social Service Departments, of creating highly specialised units and groups to carry out treatment, which would be completely within the control of the local authority, be staffed by social workers, and would exclude any personnel from outside.

It would be a great tragedy if this were to happen, because it would effectively stifle the wider involvement of the community which is one of the more important elements of the initial concept. Coupled with this tendency has been a parallel one which has served to dilute the original concept, by widening the idea to include all remedial and preventive work with particular groups of youngsters. The fact that Intermediate Treatment is part of that work, is evident, but to lose sight of its particular application within the wider general approach would be regrettable. Especially if it meant that the work was incorporated into the general work of the social services without reaching out to seek co-operation from other organisations in the community which could make a contribution, be of help, and possibly extend the area of dialogue between all other agencies and the social services.

The emphasis also has been subtly changed in some quarters; the original idea was to contain the youngster within the community while attempting certain forms of treatment—for some local authorities, if one is to judge by their proposals, the containment aspect has swamped the others. If the scheme is not something more than containment, then, in fact, the idea has failed; the positive element could most usefully be brought to bear upon particular youngsters from the other agencies in the community, of which the Youth Service is an important part.

Special provision, beyond the range and scope of what is available to ordinary youngsters in the community, is defeating the object of Intermediate Treatment, which was intended to hold the child within the community and find him a valid place with his contemporaries and others in local life. The more a boy or girl is subjected to 'special' treatment, in forms of specially devised provision, as a regular part of Intermediate Treatment, the farther we depart from the original concept.

I have already mentioned that the wide variety of approaches possible under the terms of the concept can be stimulating, enabling a personalised scheme to be devised, with imaginative skill, to meet particular needs. Nevertheless, such approaches must remain within the bounds of what is possible and practicable, and what is normally available within the community—to go beyond that means we are merely creating another category based around a particular form of treatment and establishing something which will become another routine approach in the future.

Nearly all initiatives seem to offer much in the early stages; those who undertake them are fired with pioneering enthusiasm, and use their imagination in improvising new techniques and devising new resources. The first promise dies with the establishment of routine; over-specialisation in the initial approach would rapidly create the sour conditions in which the first impulse and enthusiasm dies away and the concept is soon stale and regarded as another failed device.

Wide involvement by a continually changing selection of people and organisations is essential if something of the initial enthusiasm and imagination is to be kept alive—that is why over specialisation is particularly dangerous.

It has danger in another sense, also; we need to keep the community sympathetic to the development of all forms of treatment within it, and it would be dangerous to make it seem that bad behaviour led to specialist provision of a sort which was not available also to the non-delinquent children and young people in the community. Every theoretician could make a case for this compensating attitude; the public, on whose special goodwill we will depend, might not appreciate the case quite so easily in relation to this particular concept. Whether the professional staff like this fact or not, it is still important.

Selecting youngsters for Intermediate Treatment groups, without involving them in the life of the community, is self-defeating. They have already been selected too many times in different ways, to their detriment. This is not to deny that there may be special needs to be met early in the life of an order. The most obvious is for diagnostic assessment, the discovery of what I have called 'interest hooks' and the definition of certain problem areas.

It is obvious that such an assessment must be carried out early in the life of an order; it is the essential piece of work which would enable a suitable programme of associations and treatment to be devised. With certain difficult cases this might well mean the use of a special unit or group, but even here the resources of the community ought to be involved, where possible.

Many community organisations and other associations already run programmes which are intended to bring youngsters into contact with new groupings of contemporaries and new sorts of experience. These should be explored for availability first and used wherever possible. 'Venture weeks', run by the National Association of Boys' Clubs, special week-end schemes run by other organisations, and a multitude of similar activities could be used: all these provide a means of studying youngsters mixing with their contemporaries in different surroundings. Those most skilful at organising these expeditions and courses are youth-leaders, club-leaders, scout-leaders and others; if it is not felt that they would be capable of making a sufficiently skilled assessment then social workers could join in and be on the spot to do that part of the work.

In some experimental work done in this fashion some interesting attitudes emerged. Social workers, accompanying just such a course for the most part seemed to desire a one-to-one relationship with the youngsters, even within a group process; they felt more at ease and comfortable with such a situation. Club-leaders and youth-workers, on the other hand, tended to avoid the one-to-one situation and chose to work with groups of youngsters of various sizes, and it was obvious that they felt most at ease and comfortable with a group around them. There are good reasons in the background and training of the two professional groups why this should be so, especially in the context of organised venture expeditions and courses. Youth-leaders, by and large, are used to pitching tents, organising meals and site routines for parties of youngsters, whereas, as I have observed, social workers, while sometimes enthusiastic, have great difficulty in getting a tent pitched and a meal prepared.

There is also the fact that the youngsters will want to test the expertise of adults on occasions like this, and social workers are not necessarily able to meet the practical challenge in the way many youth workers are trained to do. These may seem small matters, but in the dynamic of group working, they may be significant. Of course, incapacity can be turned to advantage, but it can also create problems of leadership in what are testing circumstances, and can lead to serious problems. The best solution would be to combine the skills of the social work side and the youth-leader side.

Indeed, in some work in which I took part in the role of observer, this combination worked well. Both sides, working alongside one another in a practical situation, learned to respect the particular skills and expertise of the other, and each learned something from the other. This would be one of the main values of such co-operation, an infusion from both sides of an understanding of the role of the other.

It is surprising (it certainly surprised me) how much can emerge from such an expedition. The capacity of small groups to determine their own leadership is of considerable interest and import. During one such week the small party was divided into two groups without allocating any particular responsibility to any particular individual in either group. But spokesmen emerged.

The quieter, probably more intelligent, youngsters tended to be slightly overwhelmed and not come to the fore initially. Indeed, most of the talking, in one group, was done by one extrovert individual who happened, also, to possess the loudest voice and the determination to make it heard. The dominance of this youngster began to disappear as the group became involved in practical tasks, and after two days the noisy spokesman's authority began to wane, as the effectiveness of a quieter member of the group made itself evident.

As this happened, so the loud-voiced boy's voice began to fail him. He did not lose his voice then his authority—the situation was the reverse. There was a short period of crisis with this boy, and a little upset; but showing concern about his loss of voice, with some minor medication, and giving individual attention without comment, enabled him to withdraw with dignity and find a new role in the group, when his voice returned, but never quite so aggressively loud.

For most of these youngsters the most valuable experience was a small achievement and recognition of it during the week. A quiet word of praise for effort (not necessarily achievement) was savoured with such exquisite appreciation that the lack of such words in past experience was made poignantly obvious. The skilled encouragement of the youth workers was very important for many of the youngsters, as was their working together as a team; the capacity of those more skilled at certain tasks to turn back and help some of the less skilled developed as the week went on, and was most impressive.

One of the more important activities was the opportunity to discuss—this again seemed to be something that had been pointedly lacking in their experience and something which, for the most part, they took to with relish. The usual sex matters always received a good deal of ventilation, but not to the exclusion of other topics. Indeed some discussions on sex were launched as a form of challenge to the adults—when they refused to react with outrage, perturbation, affront or alarm, the topic rapidly lost interest, except on a straightforward, informative level. A great deal of the problems of adolescence, both emotional and practical, were aired. And useful insights into attitudes to school, work and modern society emerged.

What was most touching was the memory of any adult, no matter how marginal to the lives of the youngsters, who had, at any stage, been 'kind'—interested? concerned? of practical help? available? realistic? friendly?—and the striking way in which some seemingly trivial example of this was vividly recalled. These people, glimpsed only for a moment sometimes, in the panorama of the child's life, had remained as important presences in their recollection; many times they would say it was a pity that 'so-and-so' was not there to share some thought or experience, or they would tell stories of how this particular person had been kind. These remembered individuals ranged over the whole gamut of people with whom they were likely to come into contact —a particular social worker, a policeman, a probation officer, a teacher, a club-leader, or an ordinary member of the public or a relation, who would probably have difficulty in recalling the youngster, and much more difficulty in recalling the incident that had made them important in the youngster's memory.

Many of the incidents of kindness would, themselves, seem trivial in the extreme (especially to adults) but the youngsters shared their reminiscences, and, indeed, vied with one another in discovering such individuals, and all of them seemed to understand how important these small happenings were in the lives of the others.

This would justify, in some measure, the basic approach of Intermediate Treatment as I see it—and my views, in part, were coloured by this experience and others like it, which serve to reinforce the same sort of observations. The need to bring youngsters into contact with people who are significant and can be regarded as friendly. Another important reaction also emerged through chance.

It happened that on one site, where we had arrived with our group of youngsters, we were followed after two days by another party. We had had some initial trouble, with our own group, during the settling-in period, with obscenities launched too loudly and indiscriminately and a certain amount of fighting and rough-play. The arrival of the new group made our group discover its identity.

We, that is, the adults, were a little worried, because the new-comers were handicapped children, some physically, some mentally, and some both. During our own settling-in period we had seen how one member of our group, while a sort of pecking-order was being established, would be picked on; the others attempted to score off this individual in ways which, to an adult suscepti-bility, seemed cruel—part, perhaps, of normal adolescent ex-changes, but unfamiliar to our ears, as the order of precedence within the group was established.

The search, within our group, for butts, never extended to the newcomers. The first noticeable difference in behaviour was the modification of language within earshot of any member of the other party. The next was the modification of behaviour. Our own party, absolutely spontaneously, was quickly involved with the problems of the physically handicapped, almost over-eager in their desire to help. More touching was their concern for the mentally handicapped, even though some of this group would have offered them objects by which they might have reassured themselves about their own superiority. Never once did any member of our group seek to take advantage of the other party—at all times they were helpful and concerned.

We had to adjust our own programme to enable our youngsters to help the newcomers. There was much talk about the nature of handicaps, why they were caused, and genuine concern about the youngsters in the other party. The adults felt a little ashamed, after a short while, about their own misgivings. The capacity to show concern and demonstrate tenderness seemed very important to many of the youngsters; they would even make jokes about it, which indicated their own uneasiness in this unfamiliar role, which in no way matched the 'tough' image they had felt it obligatory to present to the world previously.

There is a whole field of emotional response to work through in childhood and adolescence which many children never fully explore, for various reasons. Tenderness is not seen as a particularly masculine quality by adolescents trying to establish their emergent male personality—and lack of it is a marked defect in many delinquent adolescent girls, in the same way.

This opportunity to show concern and a degree of caring was undoubtedly important to most of these youngsters; it is something which should be taken into account in any programme for Intermediate Treatment. The opportunity to do something for others, who appreciate it and voice their thanks, instead of always having things done to them, was of great value. Intermediate Treatment could provide many opportunities for this sort of experience in the lives of such youngsters; the most important thing is that it should not be assumed, because a child chooses to present a tough image or a hard carapace to the world, that this is not a way of reaching him or her.

This point again emphasises the need for involvement with the community; many youth organisations and clubs have evolved programmes of help in hospitals, old people's homes and for handicapped groups—this is a most important element in any scheme of Intermediate Treatment.

It was also observable how these tough youngsters responded to animals. We heard the usual stories of how parents would not allow pets, of the impossibility of keeping a dog in high-rise flats. In contact with animals—dogs, cats, horses (there was some suspicion of cows: every cow was a bull in our urban youngsters' eyes!)—a great deal of tenderness was shown, and an injured bird became the object of concern of the whole group. This, I think, has some relevance to some of the more distressing cases of cruelty to animals, and indeed to human beings, which from time to time hit the newspaper headlines. These cases are far from typical, and indeed may be responses to deprivation of the kind referred to earlier in the case of the youngster who inflicted savage injury on some horses.

Any effort to create a dimension of tenderness in the youngsters is worthwhile; where it is not possible for them to accept concern for other humans, animals may be useful in providing a first sensitizing agent, so that the capacity may have play and room to develop. Sometimes these incapacities are unrealised, because they have never had opportunity to develop; other incapacities can be just as important and crippling.

One of our own boys, who had tried to hide from the others the fact that he could scarcely read, quickly became involved with a group trying to help some of the handicapped children with similar problems; he listened on the first day, and then began to try to help. He made rapid progress, and was obviously on his way to acquiring literacy himself. This was again an important by-product of an accidental meeting.

This difficulty is not confined to difficult adolescents; we are all incapable of facing our own deficiencies, admitting to them and undertaking the necessary effort to make them good. In this situation the youngster was able to face his own problems and begin to do something about them while helping others, even worse off than himself.

A week, or even a week-end, of this sort could be valuable in schemes of Intermediate Treatment; much was learned by the adults, and as much by the youngsters. The failing of our own particular experiments was that the follow-up was not good. But that aspect of communication should be taken care of when the various organisations and the Social Services Departments learn to speak to one another more frankly and fully, as they must if Intermediate Treatment is to be meaningful.

The happy chances of these encounters emphasises how important flexibility of approach must be—in a too carefully prepared scheme there is no room for such chance encounters and insights, and little opportunity to exploit them when they occur. Only through an eclectic and co-operative approach, involving other agencies and the community at large, can the scope be created for these interactions to take place and for new insights to emerge. Only in this way can the schemes be continually refreshed and the danger of routine approaches be avoided, by which spontaneity is lost.

It also demonstrates how different the picture of a youngster can be in different circumstances and surroundings. Special units, devised for intensive diagnosis, will quickly develop their own process, and the children and young people will be made to conform to it. It will tend to get the answers its organisation predicates.

More spontaneous and less structured (perhaps I should say, less obviously structured) courses allow for more open responses from the youngsters and the discovery of hidden and possibly unexpected aspects of dimensions of personality. This is particularly valuable if the observation and assessment are made by adults who are also taking part in the activities; the more varied their own backgrounds the more valuable the final assessment is likely to be. The important thing is that they are involved— even though this goes against certain professional attitudes of the moment.

The ideal structure for such courses would seem to be a course organiser and leader, with a youth worker leading each group, assisted by a social worker—the social worker would have another function, not apparent to the youngsters, of observing, collecting information and compiling the basic material for the individual assessment. This technique, reinforced by continual exchanges of information and discussion between the adults, creates a surprisingly detailed picture of the individual youngster within a very short time.

The possibility for modifying attitudes and behaviour even in such a short time is also considerable, particularly if the liaison and follow-up were better than we were able to arrange. Though this aspect of such courses was striking, the change in some of the adults, particularly the social workers, was even more so.

One social worker, after a week with a couple of his youngsters, amongst others, commented that he knew more about his 'kids' (even though, quite deliberately, he had been attached to another group during the week) than ever before. He had an entirely new view of them, and had seen many opportunities of working with them in new and different ways, in the future. It was not really surprising, because, in that week, he had seen more of the youngsters than possibly in a year of ordinary supervisory contact, whether in the youngsters' own homes or in the offices of the Social Services Department.

Many social workers with whom I have discussed these experiences are interested but object that they do not have the time to follow through cases in this way. The pressures on them are well known. Yet, I suggest, some experience of this sort would be a refreshment to them, and probably make them more effective, not only with the youngster they accompanied on a course, but with many other clients as well.

And, indeed, if they are under such pressure, the need for calling upon the services and facilities of other organisations is emphasised. It is very often those who make the point about pressure who are also most concerned to keep Intermediate Treatment exclusively within the social worker's control. Which suggests that there are other factors at work besides pressure.

The creation of such weeks and similar courses within the structure of Intermediate Treatment seems to be indicated by the legislation—the provision of the possibility of a number of days away from home which can be made part of the conditions of the order.

It would seem to be immensely beneficial to involve chosen youngsters in such courses, and possibly repeat the experience in more than one year, where the order extends that long. Then there is a chance to assess the youngsters and to observe their progress.

If this sort of experience can be followed through by associating the child with a club, youth centre, scout troop or some other organisation in the community, preferably in contact with some adult that the youngster has met during the course, the prospects for treatment would be enhanced.

It is not possible for me to prescribe in detail just how these matters should be arranged; what I am concerned to do is to show that a few opportunities have presented themselves within my limited experience—I am sure there are many more, of much greater benefit, which can be devised by people with much wider experience and more detailed understanding and involvement than myself.

I must return, in conclusion (almost *ad nauseam*) to the need for co-operation. This has been a continuing theme; in the field of Intermediate Treatment it is particularly highlighted.

12

Other Sources of Help

The original guidance document on Intermediate Treatment issued from the Department of Health and Social Security listed certain forms of facility and activity which it felt would be of value.

Physical education, competitive sports or games, adventure training, camping, cycling, walking, climbing, sailing, boating, canoeing, riding, swimming, amateur dramatics, arts, crafts, music, dancing, remedial education, further education, evening classes, vocational education, group counselling, group discussion, debating, attendance at lectures and talks, first-aid, training in survival or rescue techniques, community or social services projects, charity fund-raising projects, pursuit of hobbies, work experience.

One large section of this catalogue is concerned with the education services, where Intermediate Treatment is seen as having potential for making good the lack of basic skills. This emphasises the need for schemes to be integrated wherever possible with the Education Department of the local authority. For many children, learning to escape from illiteracy would dispel a large part of their problem. Many informal groups and societies exist to try to help youngsters catch up in reading; these work outside the school and formal class-room atmosphere. Where they exist, they should be sought out and their help requested.

It should also be possible, and important, to bring the school into this work, either through individual teachers and through use of the school premises outside normal school hours. Though it must be emphasised that the school is not the best place in which to try to help some of these youngsters, when their school experience has been particularly unrewarding. Numbers of teachers already undertake work of this kind in various outside organisations, some attached to youth clubs, some in

143

evening classes and some in more informal groupings. Others, with proper recognition, might wish to do so; so would some retired teachers. They would be invaluable where they were available.

The school itself could also provide a focal point for activities designed for children of school age, where many youth clubs are not geared to cope. If this process developed as a result of Intermediate Treatment it would help re-define the relevance and place of schools in the local community.

This idea would not be acceptable to all head-teachers, as some of them have made clear; there are, however, many with active and involved Parent-Teacher Associations who do show a desire to help—and their Associations give access to more men and women of goodwill in the community, who understand the community's problems, and could also be of help.

The Intermediate Treatment officer should be aware of these possible reservoirs of help, and should familiarise himself, in collaboration with the School Welfare Officers, with the local schools, their staff and parents.

The Probation Service, in the past, formed many useful contacts in this way, and still uses many of them; the social workers should be alive to the same opportunities in their own work in the future.

Various head-teachers, aware of needs in their own community, organise informal after-school play-groups, with the help of members of staff and parents, to care for children whose parents are both working and who do not return home until one or two hours after formal schooling has ended for the day. This period in the child's daily life is one of high risk when he faces this situation. This local initiative, born of a recognised need, could be developed with great advantage in many areas.

Again I am aware that we are on sensitive territory—the border regions between various professions, professional bodies and skills—but since the failure of the child is one which has emerged from a generalised situation, it is wrong to insist upon compartmentalisation of the attempts to deal with it. There is a widespread need for this form of direct preventive work; Intermediate Treatment, even with its limitations, could create the necessary conditions and understanding to enable this co-operation to develop and expand.

There are various groups which attempt to help truants and

school-refusers, drawing on different skills and insights; where their good will can be won, they would be important in any Intermediate Treatment scheme. Many settlements, voluntary organisations, and local groups are involved in this work—without impinging upon their independence, their capacity to experiment and their particular identity, their effectiveness could be enhanced if their resources were understood, supported and properly used.

The resources of the local police should never be overlooked in this context by those responsible for formulating Intermediate Treatment schemes. There are obvious difficulties and areas of sensitivity—there are also obvious advantages and opportunities. Many police forces know their communities well, and, apart from their police function, also have useful knowledge through their Juvenile Bureaux and Community Relations schemes. Moreover, many policemen, despite certain stereotype views of the force, have a deep understanding of the problems; they are not all concerned with 'nicking as many kids as possible'.

Most police forces have good sporting facilities available, and many policemen are skilled in various sports; the police cadets, in particular, have always been a good source of helpers on expeditions, adventure courses and other activities of this kind. Many of them are interested in, and willing to help with, the training of youngsters.

Numbers of police forces, and individual members of those forces, have been involved with clubs and other activities through the years; they provide, like other bodies of citizens, a reservoir of resources, where their interest and enthusiasm can be aroused. Many police forces are eager to enter into this role, where they are given the opportunity.

Some police officers would not like the idea; some social workers would regard it with equal distaste. Both groups can agree to remain outside any work of this kind. But where police officers do become involved, they can be a very important and useful nucleus for many possible activities within the scope of Intermediate Treatment. They bring their own qualities to the work which could prove beneficial and advantageous.

Another group of activities referred to by the Department of Health and Social Services booklet is of particular relevance and importance. This is the reference to community and social work projects. There are organisations in most communities whose

concern is to make good certain deficiencies in community provision and to help cope with certain problems in respect of the
old, the handicapped and others in need. The involvement of
certain youngsters on Intermediate Treatment in this sort of
project could be very valuable indeed.

Some people react with horror to this sort of suggestion, for
no very good reason; the anecdote I recounted in the last chapter,
where a group of tough teenagers were brought into contact with
a group of handicapped people shows clearly the mutual benefits
which might accrue.

The capability to be of service, with the improvement in self-
esteem and the enhancement of the self-image this can bring, is
likely to prove a key factor in helping certain youngsters. Many
clubs and schools already organise activities on these lines.
Youngsters are keen and active members of organisations asso-
ciated with hospitals and other institutions which cater for the
handicapped and the less able in our community.

Work of this kind is socialising and sensitising; these are in-
gredients that we are seeking to restore to the life experience of
many youngsters. The effectiveness of the Community Service
Orders for an older age-group illustrates the usefulness of such
an approach for the younger age-group, where potentially it is
even more valuable. The people who assume responsibility for
these schemes are aware of the difficulties and possible dilemmas;
they would be best able to advise individual social workers about
the prospects of success with a particular subject.

Many boys' clubs and youth clubs also organise projects of
this kind, and help out also in fund-raising schemes. These are all
effective forms of activity and potentially beneficial. In most
communities where every resource is under pressure, and many
statutory and voluntary bodies are under strain, this voluntary
effort should be encouraged, for it is doubly beneficial. The involvement of youngsters within the compass of Intermediate
Treatment would be an addition to the community's resources,
as well as the experience proving advantageous to the youngsters.
There is not only the fact that they can be of service, which is
important, but the possibility of creating new perspectives in
their view of their own problems and the problems of others.

This form of ongoing involvement directly in the community,
coupled with the more orthodox involvement in clubs and youth

organisations, would give a new dimension to Intermediate Treatment.

Where there is a teacher-training college or any institution of higher education available to the community, the resources should always be investigated. Students who are going on to become teachers could bring much to schemes with which they are involved. Other students, who might be intending to do social work, become lawyers or doctors, or enter any other profession, would be invaluable; it would help their own growth in understanding while bringing youngsters into contact with committed, thoughtful, concerned and articulate people, not much older than themselves, with a wider life experience and outlook, who are developing their own particular skills.

There are clubs and associations within most polytechnics and colleges which might wish to welcome a youngster or two into their activities—the danger that such youngsters might be conspicuous can be overcome with a little care and discretion, if the will is there. The intellectual, artistic and social stimulation which such contacts could provide would be of particular value to certain youngsters.

Theatre clubs, amateur dramatic societies, amateur film societies (concerned with making as well as studying and showing film), literary societies, art societies, local orchestras and musical societies are all important resources. Many clubs also have lively and interested groups working in these same areas. In the National Association of Boys' Clubs, for instance, there is as much emphasis on these activities as there is on sport and the more obvious forms of interest.

It is important to emphasise the need for these forms of interest and pursuits to set alongside the obvious physical activities which should be provided for. There is no doubt that many youngsters require physical challenge and stimulation. The fact is that it is often easier to provide this form of involvement, but this must not be allowed to conceal the need for intellectual, mental and spiritual stimulation and challenge as well.

One interesting aspect of the provision of physical pursuits is the tendency for youngsters to welcome those in which there is an element of risk present, such as motor-cycling, cross-country riding, potholing, climbing and expeditions—possibly these forms of risk-taking are in compensation for the loss of other forms of risk-activity, where the chief danger is of involvement with the

law. The acquisition of skills is important in itself; it enhances
the youngster's self-image. The creation of new skills or the
enhancement or development of old, whether physical or mental,
are worthwhile aims in any scheme of treatment.

Local authority Social Services Departments have taken different attitudes towards Intermediate Treatment. Not all authorities have yet appointed an Intermediate Treatment officer, others
have merely added this job to that of an existing worker. The
courts, also, have varied in their attitude to making orders, some
showing far more willingness than others to have recourse to
Intermediate Treatment.

Various reasons are given for the dilatoriness on the part of
some of those responsible. One or two authorities have stated
that they do not wish to appoint an Intermediate Treatment
officer until they have facilities available beyond the already
existing range of facilities in the community—this would seem to
be defeating one of the main aims of the order. Those who hold
this view argue that most of the facilities already available have
been tried and rejected by those who might be made subject to
Intermediate Treatment orders. I have indicated earlier the reluctance of some youngsters to become involved in services and
activities which they believe are not intended for them, and the
existence of such a group of youngsters largely invalidates this
line of argument.

The other argument is one I have already touched upon—
the element of compulsion. This objection is raised by social
workers on the one side and youth workers on the other. Again,
as I have shown, this element of compulsion can be important—
it is a way of winning involvement in the first instance, and if it is
used properly it can lead on to more constructive, voluntary
associations afterwards, where there is a good scheme in operation.

Most local authorities seem to have been more enterprising
than this. Many have shown a great deal of boldness and imagination. One London borough, for instance, has linked up with a
scheme in its area where small groups work from a central base
on schemes which they devise for themselves. The first programme
has involved the following activities: youth hostelling, dry-skiing,
rowing, riding, letter-writing, cooking, helping the handicapped,
football and planned visits to exhibitions and other places of
interest.

Another borough has joined with a centre where counselling is available in parallel with a number of the more usual club activities, and time is spent in each. Many other youngsters are already showing an interest in fieldcraft courses, archaeological digs, and schemes where practical help is given to other organisations within the borough.

Nor is the problem of employment neglected. One local authority has made contact with a number of local employers who have been won over to their scheme of Intermediate Treatment. The youngsters have been found work with these employers, for four days a week. They spend the fifth day at a centre where they discuss their problems and all aspects of their lives, and also talk out the problems of the work situation. The local authority concerned is making payments to the youngsters; these are stopped immediately they fail to attend and play a full part in the activities.

Involvement with work schemes, literacy schemes and education projects generally seem to be popular with a wide range of local authorities. One local authority is establishing small local groups, of not more than five people, led by what they call a 'linker', who are engaged in practical activities such as decorating, mechanical repairs, cooking and some general handyman activities. The National Association for the Care and Rehabilitation of Offenders is joining in this scheme.

In other schemes the emergence of interested groups, offering opportunities for involving youngsters in their activities, is noteworthy. The resources are available if they are searched out and made aware of the contribution that can be made. All these activities are aimed at giving the youngsters more confidence by enabling them to do something positive and practical.

The creation of any form of competence is important and valuable in the lives of damaged children; any possibility of achievement is worth exploring. The needs of many of the more withdrawn youngsters also require investigation and careful consideration. For them involvement is not always enough or even the most suitable approach initially. Indeed, unthinking, premature attempts at involvement may well be self-defeating. Any activity which will create new confidence and restore their self-image is important and beneficial; finding ways to do this within the community may be more difficult.

The primary need, probably, is for involvement with some sympathetic adult and the gradual and careful introduction into some compatible form of group activity in good time. The hurly-burly and the general business of the average club is not always, nor even often, the best first answer.

Such youngsters are often late to come to notice, and when discovered pose particular and special problems for any scheme of treatment. They are much more likely to be 'loners'. But if the personalisation of Intermediate Treatment is a reality, it is important to discover resources and individuals within the community who can help with these particular cases.

The need to discover 'interest hooks' becomes very important in respect of these youngsters. The difficulty will be to match the youngster, through the 'interest hook', with an organisation or an individual who is able and willing to help in a particularly dis-criminating and sensitive way, and can be trusted to do so.

The guidance issued by the Department of Health and Social Security draws attention to the needs of these youngsters:

> Some types of treatment will involve group activities, and will take place in clubs and societies, or in groups of other kinds. They may involve membership of organisations for the young which engage in a variety of activities, or of community service organisations. But there will be some children who may not be able to cope with groups or group activities, but whose need may be rather to develop some particular interest of an indivi-dual nature—perhaps an artistic interest or a hobby. Schemes will need to include provision for such children, and here there may be special scope for individual volunteers, who are willing, for example, to give instruction to a few children in particular subjects. Again there may be other children whose needs would be best met by group counselling or group therapy sessions.

After the Intermediate Treatment officer has compiled a record of the clubs and organisations within his community, he should be able to establish contact with individuals within those organisations, or known to those organisations, who would be of particular help in this direction. It would very much depend on the reaction of a particular individual, the social workers and the youngster, to each other. Any scheme has to be flexible enough to be able to incorporate these relationships if it is to be of real use.

It would be particularly valuable, where time allows, for a record of particular interests and individuals to be compiled and kept up-to-date, so that these people might be called upon if need arose. In the past, voluntary relationships of this sort, centred upon a shared interest or enthusiasm, have been highly fruitful and rewarding—the more esoteric the interest, the greater the enthusiasm and the more likely is success.

Obvious interests readily suggest themselves: stamp and coin collecting, record collecting and any other form of collecting which attracts enthusiasts (and there are very many); interests in animals of all sorts from many different standpoints—dogs, snakes, monkeys, cats, pigeons, horses, other reptiles—and also fish. Conservation groups, archaeological societies, historical societies, conservations and amenity groups would usually welcome practical help and involvement—and this could lead on to worthwhile and stimulating relationships. The opportunities are endless, if the community is properly explored and the concept of treatment is approached imaginatively.

It becomes apparent that the Intermediate Treatment officer must know his community from a rather different standpoint from his normal professional stance; he needs to look with fresh eyes to discover the unexpected and less obvious resources that may be found there. Many differing types of people in the community may be valuable sources of information—the local clergy, doctors and other professional groups, staff working out of the local authority offices in other departments, Trade Union branch secretaries and officials, civic societies, amenity societies, Rotarians, the Women's Voluntary Services, Women's Institutes and any other groups who play some significant part in the life of the community, including the secretaries and officials of all the organisations existing in the community.

Contacts of this sort are important for more than information or the provision of help for specific aspects of training or individual youngsters; they provide information channels which are two-way. The work of the Intermediate Treatment officer, if it is to be effective, can be percolated into the community through these channels. In this way, people who may mould attitudes and opinion within the community can be won over to active interest and support, which, at certain times, may be critical for success.

The need to create sympathy and understanding for the methods, aims and practice of Intermediate Treatment will prove vital to the success of any scheme, especially when, as is inevitable, things go wrong on occasion. But such understanding has wider implications. From such contacts a general understanding of the role and methods of the Social Services Department may develop, and this is important to the working of the whole of the 1969 Act, and can reinforce the work of the department in all its various fields.

Community involvement must be informed involvement; Intermediate Treatment, with its opportunity for practical working together, could be a way of informing public opinion in a very positive way. It removes the debate from a philosophical to a practical level, and may lead to positive changes of attitude in the community which could be of value.

Every person involved in Intermediate Treatment becomes an ambassador for the concept of social work; this will be important when the inevitable difficulties occur. If community concern is to be something more than lip-service and a generalised attitude, the involvement of the community must be worked for. A too rigid professional attitude towards this involvement would, in the long term, be self-defeating.

The creation of new resources and involvement of members of the public is part of community activation, part of the aim of the Social Services Department, when social workers cease to be firemen and have time to address themselves to the general health of the community in social terms.

Even within the present conditions of great pressure on the professional resources of the departments, calling upon these extra resources, in the way suggested, helps bring ordinary men and women into a constructive relationship with the local authority, shows them ways in which they can be something more than electors, who might or might not vote every so many years, and gives them some view of the areas of concern in the community and familiarises them with ways in which they may begin to play a more active part in the community.

If, especially in the urban context, we are to see this revitalisation of community and civic life, then any form of activity which tends towards this end is of value, and involvement of individuals in the ways indicated has implications at many different levels. We are finally concerned not only with the sensitisation of individual youngsters, but the positive sensitisation of the community.

I hope I have been able to justify some part of the importance

I attach to Intermediate Treatment. I trust that the bored reactions I have heard on various occasions from different professional people when talking about the concept do not prevail: 'We've heard all this before. This is just the latest panacea. It will go the way of all the other panaceas.' If it does, of course, the concept will fail. It is important, however, to emphasise that no one claims that Intermediate Treatment is a panacea; it is a device, but one with interesting and stimulating potential, nothing more.

If the approach fails in this form, many other forms of important work in the community will also be placed in jeopardy, and that would be a considerable setback to the developing concerns of social work. The move back to the community to deal with particular problems which, in part, the community has created, will lose ground. That would mean the continuance of institutional forms of treatment in many areas of concern where it is, patently, not the best answer, and the continuance, out of desperation, of policies which have already been proved not to be successful. The use of institutional care should be on a much narrower front, directed at particular and special problems, because of the additional problems that all institutional provision brings in its wake.

Intermediate Treatment is one way in which this change of direction and emphasis can be given validation and proved to be viable. The failure would extend beyond the provision for youngsters over the whole field of methods of care and penal reform. Anyone who does not wholeheartedly work for the success of Intermediate Treatment should be aware of the far-reaching consequences of failure, and the device should rank high in concern.

There is no guarantee that Intermediate Treatment will be effective. Unless it is approached with full appreciation of the potential, with imaginative flexibility and determination, it cannot succeed. I will repeat that it is not a panacea—there are none in this field.

It is another instrument to make good some of the defects in individual experience and community life. It could reach into the community in ways which, if properly exploited, could be significant, and it does have implications for the development of social service which reach far beyond its immediate, important, but limited, objectives.

For those who talk, in general terms, of the concrete jungles of our inner cities and urban areas, deplore the lack of colour and vitality of lives lived in the twilight areas and the shadow of highrise blocks, who deplore the bleeding away of local resources, energy and initiatives, and who then settle down into genteel professional despair, my arguments are not likely to rouse much enthusiasm.

But for those who are concerned, over a wide front, to do something about the quality of our life nationally, locally and individually, and who can see some sense in new beginnings (no matter how small) I suggest that Intermediate Treatment does hold some promise. I hope that it will succeed and that the by-products of that success will enable us to devise further techniques along similar lines in the future, for other groups of people with problems. These new departures will have to be built on what is learned during the development of Intermediate Treatment during the next few years.

What other device of recent years has offered the potential that Intermediate Treatment contains: the uncovering of new resources and energies within the community: the closer association of many of the organisations working within the community; the beginnings of the revitalisation of many of our inner urban communities? For these reasons it should win support. It is also deserving of support for the benefits it could bring to a large number of youngsters in keeping them out of institutional care and holding them within the community, to return to the mainstream of community life and experience.

13

Immigrant Children

Pigmentation is a real problem in the juvenile courts and the administration of the 1969 Act. I have chosen the word as the least emotive available. On the simplest level the coloured youngster feels particularly conspicuous in a court, surrounded by white faces. The row of white faces must confirm the belief that many disturbed young coloured people have that the law is a white institution, intended only for whites.

Some attention has been given to the coloured community in our midst by the appointment of a few coloured magistrates and court officers, but this is a slow process. And there are many people who would argue that appointment on the basis of colour is wrong. Those people I have encountered have been of the highest quality, and have well deserved appointment on the basis of the contribution they can make to the court's working. Even that sounds slightly condescending, and indicates some of the difficulties in writing about this topic at all.

Perhaps it is due to this that many people avoid discussing the problem in relation to the courts and the legal process, because these matters present particular difficulties. Some claim that there can be no problem, because all are equal before the law. This is a splendidly idealistic attitude; it has very little relevance to the real situation in the courts at the moment. Very often such arguments are used to cover a loss of nerve in face of the problem.

The issue will not go away if we pretend it is not there. In avoiding it we jeopardise the future, and miss many opportunities to establish understanding and relationships within the minority communities.

The problem is not particular to the court, but in the court setting many of the problems are presented in a more naked form, where the consequences cannot easily be avoided. Most striking is the resentment that many coloured youngsters feel towards the police. The police are the agents of society, and their attitudes reflect the broad spectrum of attitudes prevalent in society towards

coloured youngsters and the coloured immigrant population
generally. Their intervention is usually into situations of greatest
stress, and their appearance on the scene can be an additional
stress factor. They cannot choose to opt out of these situations,
even if they wished to; the anger, suspicion and resentment of the
youngsters focuses upon them for this reason: they become the
representatives of the oppressive white society.

Many youngsters will claim in court that they have been unfairly picked on by the police: very often a youngster will ask,
'Why me? Why not that other kid?' The coloured youngster no
longer bothers to ask; he, or she, believes he knows.

Most coloured youngsters do not feel that they are equal before
the law, especially when, for them, the law begins and ends with
the police. Many of them believe when they arrive in court that
everything has been pre-arranged between the police and the
court; they regard the bench and the court process with scepticism. Many of them do not even wish to defend themselves,
believing nothing they will say will make any difference to the
result. They do not believe the court is willing to listen to them—
the reason being that they are not white.

They are highly sceptical of anyone who tries to tell them the
contrary. I recently heard a coloured officer trying to explain the
working of the court to a young West Indian; he was called an
Uncle Tom for his pains. When this situation applies it is obvious
that there is good reason for concern, and a great deal of work has
to be done if the law is to be meaningful to these youngsters in
any positive sense.

A young West Indian said to me: 'They'll get me for doing
nothing, on "sus" or obscene language or something, so why try
to stay out of trouble?' The danger of that attitude, and all that
it implies, needs no emphasis; yet it is commonplace amongst a
certain section of West Indian youngsters. Many of them do not
see the law as being concerned with them, except in a negative,
repressive way—it is 'Whitey Law'. The police and the court are
merely society's instruments in the racial struggle.

It is a defensive attitude, born of anger, fear, and frustration;
we must ask ourselves what is happening which allows such an
attitude to develop and gain credence with groups of coloured
youngsters.

It is true that many youngsters who are likely to find themselves
in conflict with the law adopt this attitude in one or another form.

If there is no real defence against an allegation, the easiest way out of the problem is to accuse the police of malpractice of some sort: using threats to obtain statements, manufacturing evidence, prejudice or brutality. Courts hear versions of this very frequently; sometimes it is justified, sometimes it is not. That is a matter which the court has to decide. If it does believe such an allegation, or any part of it, the consequences for the police officer concerned are very serious indeed, and all police officers are well aware of this, and are continually reminded of the fact. The bench, for its part, must be vigilant in such matters, and unflinching in its decisions.

If any meaningful dialogue is to develop in the court process, the fairness of the proceedings must be demonstrated and any ideas of prejudice or lack of impartiality between the parties dispelled. Most benches do this job as honourably and as honestly as they can. Probably they make mistakes, but it is unlikely that they would ever allow prejudice to affect their decisions. If they are doing their job properly, they will treat all who come before them alike, and I have given some indication of the care with which this has to be approached in an earlier chapter.

In one matter, however, there is need for particular care. The court must ensure that its language is properly understood at all times, but there is a particular trap when the defendants come from one of the minority communities. There are differences in pronunciation, use of words and particular forms of syntax which have to be watched carefully.

When visiting one court I heard the chairman say, unthinkingly, 'Try to speak English.' The youngster had been under the impression that he had been doing precisely that; the result was that he became confused, and finally relapsed into resentful silence. The mutual incomprehension and resultant exasperation on both sides had gone to reinforce the impression of prejudice in the youngster's mind.

One of the greatest dangers for many immigrants and their families is the fact that they come from English-speaking countries; their English not always the English of this country. This fact is important in terms of education, but it is critical on occasion in the courts. The belief that you are communicating, when this is only partially true, is a greater danger than blank incomprehension.

Many immigrant youngsters in trouble use their colour as a

retreat; they prefer to see the issue in terms other than those of the court: not of right or wrong, of an allegation made, and proved or disproved, of guilt or innocence—they prefer to see the issue as one of black versus white. This is simpler, more dramatic, and if you are confused, frightened, angry or resentful, it is an easy way out; it is ultimately destructive of individual responsibility and dignity and corrosive of human values.

'I am not here because I did anything wrong; I have been picked on because I am black.' 'I have not been found guilty because of what I did, but because of the colour of my skin.' 'I have no need to examine my behaviour, because I cannot change my colour.' These are the defensive attitudes of many minorities at many different times in history—they are accentuated when pigmentation is the issue.

These attitudes are all various forms of 'outs'. They hold a degree of validity for some youngsters because of things which happen to them in our society. In fact most of these youngsters suffer the same disadvantages as the white youngsters from the same areas—they have the additional factor of race and colour to heighten their disaffection, and a particular minority solidarity to fall back on and to give greater reinforcement to their attitudes. The sad fact is that this sort of retreat from reality, whether for reasons of survival or individual image-enhancement, ultimately contributes to further alienation. Indeed many of them seek alienation as a means of justification of their behaviour.

It would be idle to pretend that there were not prejudices—they exist, in both communities, in mirror-image form. It is better to examine the differences, and the difficulties, rather than pretend that they do not exist. If they go unchallenged, the stereotypes may develop unchallenged, and prejudice flourish uncontrolled.

Stereotypes, in all situations of conflict, are the focal point for prejudice. The majority must see beyond the stereotypes and try to understand what life is like for a youngster in our society whose attitudes, social conditioning and expectations (as well as colour) are different from our own. This is important for all youngsters; race is not the only barrier—there are others, age, generation, culture, class. But it is particularly important in respect of youngsters from other racial groups.

There are a number of basic patterns to be observed in the lives of many youngsters who appear in court from the immigrant communities. It is a familiar scenario to every juvenile court magistrate, social worker and probation officer who has to compile and study social enquiry reports on these youngsters. The fact that it is commonplace does not reduce the poignancy of the individual story.

Immigrant families are under very special pressures, apart from the problem of race. The parents have usually come to this country in an attempt to make a better life for themselves and their children, escaping from a pattern of large-scale unemployment in their home country. They are likely, therefore, to be highly motivated towards success in terms of ownership and work. Usually the father comes first; he obtains work, and works every hour of overtime he can, to save money for his wife's fare, so that she may join him. This is a period when the integrity of the family is under great stress. For some the money is never saved, or another woman comes into the life of a lonely man, and the wife never arrives. Once the money is saved and the fare sent to the wife, she leaves her children and comes to join her husband.

After mother has arrived, she obtains work, and the money is saved to provide fares for the children. Meanwhile the children are left in the care of grandparents, or aunts and uncles, or some other members of the extended family back home.

After more hard work and saving the children are sent for; sometimes they arrive all together, sometimes they come separately, as money becomes available. The children find, very often, that they are part strangers; many of them discover that they have younger brothers and sisters, born to their parents in the intervening years, who are strangers to them. Very often the younger children are objects of resentment, because they have shared the parents' lives and love at a time when the older children have been denied them. In many instances the children join one parent and a step-parent, which can be the cause of further stress and bewilderment.

The stresses, at many levels and of various kinds, which can threaten family relationships at this time, and menace its structure, as a result of this compound of experiences, need no elaboration or detailed comment.

These stresses would pose great dangers to any family group subjected to them; these particular families are in an alien country, with alien customs, and with strange, not necessarily friendly, faces all round. The older children find they have arrived in a country which lacks warmth (of all kinds) and is unfamiliar; they remember the country of their childhood, which, to them, had more colour, more security and more affection. They have arrived in what they have thought of, over many years, as the 'mother country'—they do not find the welcome they expect and are disappointed at the reaction of 'mother' to them.

The parents believed they had come to a land of opportunity; most of them arrived with a touching, not to say, flattering belief in the efficacy of the education system of this country. Many of them claim that they undertook the agonies of emigration to obtain better educational and employment opportunities for their children. Many of the children show a marked difference in attitude to the schools and job situation, even where their parents' faith persists.

The children find the schools bewildering; they quickly learn how out of step they are in many different ways. A change of school within a country and culture is recognised as a source of stress and anxiety for a child and a problem period in his development. The consequences of a move from one country to another, and arrival in a society with cultural attitudes and communal patterns in marked contrast to the society from whence they came, the difficulties of assimilation into an entirely different school system must have far-reaching effects. Many children find it hard to adjust, and valuable time, in terms of educational progress, is lost while that adjustment is made (within whatever limits of success); the immigrant children find themselves falling to the bottom of the scale of esteem within the school, desperately seeking a place in the life of the school, trying to keep up and make their way.

Even the brightest, most intelligent and most adaptable find it difficult; many others become lost and alienated.

I have already mentioned the difference in the use of English; many immigrant youngsters, who believed that they spoke English, find that their English is not the English of the schools and teachers. Their English has its own tradition, validity, virtue and vitality; it does not enjoy academic esteem. It is a variant English, often retaining words and constructions which have fallen into disuse in Great Britain, possessing its own coinages of power and expressiveness, often more colourful in its expressions and striking in its descriptive powers and rhythmic capacities. But the youngsters must accommodate themselves to a system which, by and large, still lives by one standard of 'correct' English. They have to be weaned from their own English to the English of current British usage—and there are many pitfalls in matters of emphasis, nuance and modes of expression.

These difficulties are highlighted by some recent figures from the Community Relations Commission's *Educational Needs of Children from Minority Groups*, which show that in Inner London amongst pupils transferred from primary to secondary schools assessed for competence in the use of English, immigrant children were under-represented at the top of the scale and over-represented at the bottom. Only 8 per cent of immigrant children appeared in the top quarter of the assessment scale, against 25 per cent of non-immigrant children. In the lowest quarter, 23 per cent of non-immigrant children appeared, as against 62 per cent of immigrant children. An even more marked imbalance is to be seen in the numbers of children assessed in terms of 'verbal reasoning'.

Of the various immigrant communities the most disadvantaged were the West Indian children; 9·2 per cent in the highest quarter of the scale for English, 7·4 per cent for mathematics, and 7·2 per cent for 'verbal reasoning'. Amongst children of Asian origin the comparable figures were 19·3 per cent for English, 20·2 per cent for mathematics, and 21·1 per cent for 'verbal reasoning'. For the indigenous children the figures were as follows: 25 per cent for English, 22·9 per cent for mathematics and 19·8 per cent for 'verbal reasoning'. The failure to recognise the difficulties facing immigrant children generally, and West Indian children in particular has contributed to these disparities.

There is an understandable bitterness amongst some of the older members of the West Indian community, which has communicated itself to many of the youngsters, where it tends to appear in more violent fashion. Many of the youngsters reject their parents; they refuse to accept any guidance from them, and despise their attitudes. The parents urge their children to take every opportunity in education to gain work in a trade or a profession. Many of the children recognise quite early in their lives that, coming from the areas and schools in which they find themselves, their parents' aspirations are not easily achieved, they are caught in a class-trap, added to which is the problem of race and colour.

They are made aware that they are members of a minority, a

6

conspicuous minority, with all that that implies. And so they tend to band together defensively both in school and in the community, to protect themselves, their culture, their identity. They resist assimilation because they suspect that assimilation is a fraud. Their last refuge is their racial identity, the integrity of the minority group.

They are not willing to accept some theoretical advantage from assimilation when they believe this means a dilution of their group strength in the alien society in which they find themselves. Very often the youngsters are more alert and alive to these issues than their parents, or, at least, they are far more vocal about them. Thus the potential alienation of the average adolescent is compounded in these youngsters by additional factors of stress, and the result is sometimes highly destructive both of individual integrity and social cohesion.

They find they have moved from a society which, whatever its true nature, was to them as children characterised by warmth, the care and concern of the extended family grouping, and lack of pressure, to one which is in sharp contrast to this recollected image. They mistake the tensions of growing up, and the particular problems of adolescence, as factors which only occur in the host society. They find themselves highly disadvantaged in a society which is characterised by intense competitiveness. They have moved from the 'warmth' to a community where they are made aware of stress, and where the surrounding community is at best indifferent, and may be, in many subtle ways, hostile. They have moved from a community where their colour is that of the majority to one in which it marks them out as part of the conspicuous minority. The shocks in this transition are severe and far-reaching.

These stressful factors, when joined with the 'normal' stresses of adolescence, begin to define a context in which anti-social behaviour may well manifest itself in various ways, and gain some sanction. Even for those born in this country, many of these factors are operative.

The gap between generations receives additional emphasis in their life experience. The parents mostly subscribe to the traditional values of their own country and upbringing; every immigrant group, whether West Indian, Asian or Cypriot, maintains much more patriarchal standards within the family than are usual in current attitudes in indigenous British families. The parental attitudes of most immigrant families are fundamentally more Edwardian than of our own time.

The stereotype image of the West Indian male which became current in the 'fifties, and which still lingers in some corners of our society, of a man fond of rum, somewhat feckless and uncaring, was as condescending as it was untrue. The majority of West Indian parents adopt parental attitudes which are the reverse of this. Their concern for their children, particularly when young, is real and warm. They are not so happy with their children in adolescence. Very often they become confused and angry about what happens to their children as they grow up, and particularly about the attitudes their children adopt towards them. I have seen West Indian parents in court devastated by the opinions expressed about them by their children.

Many West Indian children see their parents as people of no account, ironically adopting the standards of the host community towards their parents. The children share attitudes with their contemporaries in the wider community; their parents' attitudes seem old fashioned and irrelevant. The youngsters soon discover that white children are not subject to the restrictions that their own parents try to fasten on them; they rebel against the attempt to direct (and, as they see it, restrict) their lives. This sharpens the inevitable conflict.

Many of the parents are likely to be working long hours; many of the children are called upon to assume responsibility for domestic chores and caring for younger siblings. The ambitious parents want their children to work hard, to commit themselves completely to the work ethic. In many families both parents are working, and, more often than not, one, or both, of the parents are doing a full-time job and a part-time job as well. Usually this is to enable them to buy their own home, for they are eager house-owners, aspiring to middle-class standards in areas that conspicuously do not admit these standards for the indigenous population. The bewilderment of parents when faced with children who reject their cherished aspirations and ambitions is painful in the extreme.

When their children come into conflict with the law, their bewilderment and hurt is increased. They have lived with the idea of their children realising ambitions and achieving standards of living which have not been possible to their generation; in a sense, naturally and honourably, but sometimes damagingly, they wish their children to live out their dream.

Their aspirations are not unworthy, and, indeed, are admirable; they will say they want a child to become a doctor or a teacher when it is patently obvious (especially to the child) that this is not realistic, and is not even desired by the child. The confrontation with reality can be bitter in its consequences. They have often, unwittingly, created a new sense of failure in the child, and the result is further estrangement and disaffection.

Many of the parents belong to close-knit religious groups, with very high (if, sometimes, narrow) standards. The children in trouble have rejected these standards dramatically. Most West Indian parents personalise this failure very pointedly. They will talk of the child having 'let me down'. It is a personal affront, and cuts very deep.

The tragedy is that these same parents, concerned and caring during the hopeful phase of their child's development, can be much more ruthless in rejecting the child once he or she has fallen from grace.

Many parents, of all sorts and from all groupings, within the community, will, in an outburst of anger, say in court that they want nothing more to do with a particular child; most times this is not true. It is, however, in my experience, much more likely to be true if a West Indian parent says it. This is sad for all concerned, and creates further likelihood of damage and suffering.

The result has been that a significant number of young West Indians are cut off from their families very early in their lives, when they are far too young to fend for themselves adequately. The dangers of further alienation need no emphasis.

Some of these youngsters turn to petty crime to keep themselves alive and to have a little money in their pockets. Once they have overcome their initial reserve and suspicion they will speak of these matters with an unnerving degree of detachment and lack of concern.

The circumstances in which they find themselves provide for many of them an uneasy justification for what they do. They rationalise their behaviour with a few catch-phrases they have garnered from some of the extreme political groupings. They claim they are only redressing the balance between themselves and the rest of society, or maintain that what they do would be done to them by white members of society if they were caught on their own.

Some of them admit that they rob people for money, which

they cannot obtain any other way, because they cannot get work. Most of them claim not to want to hurt anyone. But some of them will laugh at the plight of various of their victims, and draw some pleasure from the humiliation they have inflicted on others. Some complain they were forced to use violence because their victims refused to co-operate. But one or two, the same proportion probably as in any other delinquent group, no matter what its racial constitution, seem to relish the opportunity to show their strength and inflict hurt and humiliation.

When any attempt is made to point out that their behaviour makes the relationship between the races that much more bitter, they are not prepared to give the matter consideration. For many of them, robbery is revenge; they believe themselves to be in a survival situation, and self-preservation justifies everything.

The fact that many of them claim that they only rob whites seems, in their eyes, to palliate the offence; they maintain proudly that they would never rob a 'brother', though this is not always true. This attitude certainly points up a serious problem in the field of race relations.

In fact many of their statements echo similar attitudes in young white thieves, but the white youngsters seldom justify their behaviour in terms of race, though they, in their turn, recall more easily the times they robbed Pakistanis (who, to them, are all Asians).

It must be emphasised that these activities are not confined to immigrant youngsters; there are as many white youngsters and gangs engaged in similar depredations. But whereas in the 'fifties it was a fact that, proportionately, West Indian youngsters were under-represented in delinquency statistics, every indicator shows that today they are over-represented, and this is a matter for concern. Nor can the whole picture be seen.

Many of the casual thefts from children stopped in the street or in cinemas (and, increasingly, in school) are of such small account that they are not reported, or not followed up very thoroughly. Bag snatching from older women is something which attracts much more attention.

It is significant that most of these youngsters will not talk about the robbery of older women; if asked about it, they will deny it strongly. Nor are they proud of robbing other children. Their main victims, according to them, are drunks, queers, or members of other racial minorities—Asians seem popular victims for both West Indian and white youngsters. The irony of their choice of victim—members of other minority groups—is worth noticing.

These activities add to the suspicion and distrust endemic within the community in certain areas; they confirm prejudice on both sides. West Indian youths gathered together in the street or crowding into a shop are a cause for suspicion. Very often the police are called in areas where this sort of petty crime is rife, even when the gathering is perfectly innocent. The police cannot ignore any appeal, and must be cognisant of public opinion in these matters; and for them there is always the danger of some petty incident getting out of hand and going badly wrong.

A group of youngsters merely larking about in the street or at a bus stop become angry with the police when suddenly they are descended upon, and immediately make accusations of racial victimisation. One wrong word or gesture from either side and the situation escalates into a potentially dangerous one. As a result suspicion and hostility are fed on both sides. The number of West Indian youngsters involved in criminal activities is a small minority (this cannot be emphasised too much nor too often) but their behaviour feeds anger between the races and makes a difficult situation far more dangerous.

These experiences are at the root of the West Indian youngsters' particular dislike of what they call 'sus'—a charge of being a suspected person, loitering with intent to commit a criminal offence. It is not a charge that magistrates like, because it asks the bench to read the mind of the defendant and divine his intentions, and is, in any case, lacking in specificity and always nebulous. The nature of the charge implies that no offence was committed; the evidence must always be circumstantial and derived from police observation—and it immediately opens the police wide to accusations of prejudice. Usually such cases resolve themselves into a straight conflict of evidence between the observing police officers and the accused. This charge probably creates more distress and confusion in the court, and in the families of youngsters, than any other.

The other group of charges, involving some threat to the peace, usually arise out of some horse-play or noisy confrontation in the streets. These happen all the time, but when pigmentation appears as an issue, they seem to attract more attention. Very often the youngsters involved in these incidents represent a mixture of the races on both sides; occasionally, it is true, there is some racial component in the confrontation.

The public, not unnaturally, are concerned about these incidents. They ask what the police are doing to prevent them, and guarantee the peace and safety of other members of the public in the streets. Many parents are also concerned in case their own children are drawn in and become involved, either in danger or with the law. By the time the police arrive, the situation is likely to be confused.

All the police see is a milling group of youngsters, surging back and forward, probably shouting insults and abuse, blocking the pavement and spilling over into the road; usually there is little more than gesturing and jostling going on, but the potential for nastiness is there and evident.

If anyone is wielding any form of weapon, the police will make for them; they will also try to sort out the ringleaders, in the situation as they see it. But it would appear that it is often very much a lottery who is detained and who is not.

These situations are difficult for everybody. The court has to have specific allegations proved against specific individuals. Much of the evidence about a confused situation is itself confusing. Most times the individuals finally brought to court claim to be innocent passers-by or spectators; the real ring-leaders, it is alleged, saw the police coming and were wise enough to disappear without trace before the first policeman was out of his vehicle. Very often, if what is said in court is a good guide, the police seem only to have concerned themselves with innocent spectators, and to have picked on black youngsters only.

The members of the public who summoned the police in the first instance are reluctant to come to court. If they do appear, their evidence is very often indecisive and imprecise. Every person charged in court will claim to have been picked on unfairly. The coloured youngsters are sure that this is because of their colour. It is not possible for the court to ascertain why certain youngsters were arrested and others were not; it is never possible to hear the account of those who got away. Usually the outcome is unsatisfactory all round. And each of these incidents goes to feed the myth of virulent colour prejudice amongst the police, and to feed racial prejudice.

Very often the bench is clear about only one point—that something unpleasant was happening in a public thoroughfare at a given time, and that the police had to intervene. The law requires more than that. The court has to dismiss cases because of lack of specific evidence against particular individuals. Immediately, the public complain that the court is powerless or unwilling to do anything about a scandalous situation. The fact remains that the court can only decide on substantiated facts, which stand up in court; if it moved from that position worse damage would ensue.

These matters are only glimpses of a very complex problem with many facets which create real difficulties in administering the law and maintaining order in society. The real problem is one which lies outside the province of the court and concerns what is happening to numbers of young immigrants in our society. Our failure in this field has led to embittered relationships between the police and the West Indian community, which in some areas is very near danger point. The delinquency of a number of coloured youngsters is a symptom of a much graver problem lying partially concealed.

Society as a whole has failed lamentably in acknowledging much of the problem, let alone devising ways of tackling it. Much more vigorous work needs to be done in the schools to help the disadvantaged, and much greater energy deployed in advising on employment and obtaining employment for youngsters from immigrant communities. There is need for a much more closely concerted and determined effort to tackle the numerous problems within the families of immigrants and in the areas where immigrants tend to congregate.

We recognised the cultural shock implicit in immigration much too late in the day; we were busy discussing the preservation of our own cultural standards at a time when many of these youngsters were lost, and felt abandoned, in the desert between conflicting and contrasting cultures. There is still time to repair most of the damage brought about by our own preoccupation, insensitivity and neglect, but that time is running out. If the effort is not made there could be much more serious trouble in store for the future.

14

The Juvenile Bureau

The 1969 Act compelled the police to review their charge procedure. Under the new Act, they have to consult on certain matters with the local authority before bringing a child to court.

Where care proceedings are contemplated, the agent bringing the case, whether the police, the local authority or an officer of the National Society of Prevention of Cruelty to Children, must 'reasonably believe' that the child is in need of 'care and control which he is unlikely to receive unless the court makes an order'. Thus no constable can bring a child before the court without having made sure of this provision, which, in effect, means informing and consulting with the local authority Social Services Department.

The local authority then carries out its part of the process, which is set out in the Act as follows:

> If a local authority receive information suggesting that there are grounds for bringing care proceedings in respect of a child or young person who resides or is found in their area, it shall be the duty of the local authority to cause enquiries to be made into the case, unless they are satisfied that such enquiries are unnecessary.

A similar sort of provision applies to the prosecution of young people age 14 to 17. The police officer may prosecute only if he is satisfied that 'it would not be adequate for the case to be dealt with by a parent, teacher or other person, or by means of a caution from a constable or through the exercise of the powers of the local authority or other body not involving court proceedings'.

The effect of these provisions is far reaching. There must be consultation between police and other agencies at all times. Indeed, the spirit underlying the Act, as set out in the publication, *Children in Trouble*, urges consultation between the police, magistrates and the local authority social workers, teachers and others, with the need to maintain a continuous flow of information and an examination of working procedures at all times between all of these groups.

One of the most important aspects of the provisions of the Act, so far as the police were concerned, was the recognition of the power of the police to caution offenders. The police had always had a discretion not to prosecute in certain cases; the 1969 Act made this power statutory so far as children and young persons were concerned.

Various police forces, throughout the country, had tried to initiate schemes to help children and young persons when they came into conflict with the law, or seemed in danger of doing so. Perhaps the best known was that devised by the Liverpool police during the 'fifties. Various other police forces developed similar schemes, but this initiative on the part of the police was not always welcomed by all magistrates and lawyers. The fact that the Act recognised the value of these initiatives had a marked effect on the relationship of the police, the young offender and the court.

The Metropolitan Police, whose working procedures and approach I know best, began their own experiment in this field in 1968. As a result of the White Paper, *Children in Trouble*, they introduced what they called a 'Juvenile Bureau Scheme'. The first Juvenile Bureau was operative in one police division of the metropolitan area in 1969; this was treated as an experimental departure, and was intended to discover the best method of working and to learn about any difficulties and disadvantages. Within a year the scheme had been adopted generally throughout the metropolitan area—both the courts and the police were satisfied that the scheme had considerable merit and use. From March 1969 a Juvenile Bureau had been established in each of the twenty-three divisions of the Metropolitan Police area.

When a young offender is arrested and taken to the police station, the first priority for the police is to contact the youngster's parents or guardians. Although this now is important to the Juvenile Bureau procedure, it was always necessary, because of the Home Office Memorandum Circular No. 31 of 1964, on the interrogation of children. One section reads as follows:

As far as practicable children (whether suspected of crime or not) should only be interviewed in the presence of a parent or guardian, or, in their absence, some person who is not a police officer and is of the same sex as the child. A child or young person should not be arrested or even interviewed at school, if such action can possibly be avoided. Where it is found essential to conduct the interview at school, this should be done only with the consent and in the presence of the head teacher, or his nominee.

The police had, since the issue of this circular, been under an obligation to make contact as speedily as possible with the parents; the Juvenile Bureau proceedings make this requirement a matter of police routine, which is an advantage, since the court looks with some misgiving on evidence introduced from questioning children when parents or some other responsible adult were not present.

Once the parents or guardians are present, the incident which has brought the young offender to the notice of the police is looked into as far as possible, with the youngster and the parents, and then the offender is released into the custody of parents, guardian or some other responsible adult. It is explained to them that the Juvenile Bureau procedure will be followed through. Before they leave, the parents are handed a form which explains the reasons for bringing the young offender to the police station. The parents and youngster are also given a brief explanation of the procedure which will be followed, and are told that a visit is likely to be made to them in their own home by a police officer from the Juvenile Bureau.

The arresting officer forwards a written report to the Bureau, which then undertakes its own enquiries into the matter. This is done by the officer in charge of the Bureau, which allocates one of its own officers to follow the case through. This officer first makes enquiries within the police force, by contacting the Juvenile Index at Scotland Yard. At the same time he is responsible for informing the local authority, through the Social Services Department; he also makes enquiries of the Educational Welfare Service and the Probation Service. These enquiries are made to discover if there is anything of value to be learned about the youngster or his family which will assist the officer when recommending how the offender may best be dealt with.

When all this information and any further particulars of the offence, which are capable of proof, have been gathered together, the officer then visits the juvenile and his family at his home. The interviewing officer goes to the home in plain clothes, and the interview with the juvenile must be in the presence of the parents.

This visit is undertaken to enable the officer to see for himself the youngster in his home environment, not under stress as would be the case in the police station immediately after the incident, and it enables the officer to gather any relevant and useful information from the parents about the juvenile, not only regarding the offence, but also anything which might assist in determining how to proceed, so that whatever is best for the child or young person may be done.

The officer then compiles his report, which will cover many different sorts of information: details of the family and its structure, home accommodation, the relationship of the parents to the youngster, and the youngster to the parents and other members of the family, and their attitude to the offence. The officer may also incorporate other material if he, or she, feels it is relevant, about school, or work record, any financial problems in the home or any other domestic matters which he feels may have some bearing on the committed offence. There is no compulsion upon the parents or youngster to furnish any of this information, and it is emphasised that any information so obtained is only to be used in determining the next step in the process.

The officer may be called upon to make other visits, if the parents wish reference to be made to some other person or organisation for further information about the youngster's character—this may be a youth club leader, a doctor, a schoolmaster, a clergyman or church worker, or any other person in the community who can give some useful information about the youngster. This enables a more comprehensive picture of the youngster to be obtained, and is added to the documentation before it is forwarded.

The report goes to the head of the Juvenile Bureau, who is always a Chief Inspector, who is now known in the Metropolitan Police as the Community Liaison Officer. There is one such officer in each Metropolitan Police division, and they are all responsible to a Commander in Scotland Yard who heads a division known as A.7. It is the Community Liaison Officer who decides whether a formal caution should be given or whether a summons should be issued for the juvenile to appear in court.

If this officer decides that it is right and proper in the circumstances to give a caution, there are certain basic conditions which must be fulfilled:

1. The child must admit the offence—and the offence must, in the opinion of the officer, be fully capable of proof in court, if need be. If there is any doubt in the child's or parents' minds about this, then a caution cannot be given.

2. The parents, the juvenile and anyone affected by the offence (the loser, or sufferer) must agree to this way of dealing with the matter. Again, if agreement is not forthcoming, then a caution cannot be given.

3. It must be the opinion of the Juvenile Bureau, after consultation with the Social Services Department of the local authority, and the Education Authority, and after all other enquiries have been made, that a caution would be in the best interests of the child.

4. Where two or more children are concerned together in an offence, they will be dealt with in the same way—either everyone cautioned or everyone will go to court.

The cautioning takes place with special formality in a police station and is given by a senior officer in uniform, with the parents present. No one is allowed to think that a caution is an easy way out of difficulties, and it must not be approached in that light; the situation is explained clearly to all the parties concerned. The caution is stern and it is intended to convey the disapproval of the action which brought the child to notice of the police in the first instance. No nonsense is allowed and no 'chumminess' comes through the process. The gravity of his behaviour is conveyed to the youngster, and the risks inherent in such behaviour are explained firmly; both the youngster and the parents are also given a clear account of what is likely to happen if such behaviour continues in the future and there is a further brush with the law.

In 1971 about 30 per cent of cases involving juveniles were dealt with in this way as a result of the recommendations of the Juvenile Bureaux, accounting for something between 11,000 and 12,000 cases which came to the notice of police. This meant that this number of children avoided an appearance in court.

There are obvious difficulties in this procedure. The need to be cautious in accepting an admission by the child or the parents on behalf of the child when it may seem the easiest way out is an obvious one. Most of the officers from the bureau are alert to this danger, and are most careful about it.

There is a real difficulty when a group of children are involved. One of them, most likely the ring-leader in the incident, has been in trouble before, and it becomes clear that in his case a further caution would not be very effective. This means that all the other children involved must also go to court, even where the bureau takes the view that they could have received a caution, and, in any case, were probably led astray by the previous offender in their midst.

A similar difficulty occurs where several of the children admit the offence, but one of them does not. It is obvious that this child must have a hearing, if the police wish to proceed with the charge—and again all the youngsters must attend court.

The guidelines set out earlier were agreed at the initiation of the scheme between the magistrates and the police. Various anomalies have emerged and there is a feeling on both sides that there is room for a second look at the procedure, with a view to ironing out some of these discrepancies.

There will always be problematical areas, however, wherever the lines of decision are drawn—this is unavoidable. Some part of the decision will always be subjective on the part of the investigating officer and the Community Liaison Officer. The system, however, is working well, both in London and in other urban areas where similar schemes have been introduced. It is having the good effect of keeping youngsters, who have made one mistake, out of court; a significant proportion of them never repeat any offence and so never appear at all.

Where there is a further offence, the youngster will appear in a court, and in the end the court procedure will follow. No scheme can claim complete success, but this scheme has advantages for numbers of youngsters and their families, and removes some pressure from the court.

The Juvenile Bureau in the Metropolitan area has become part of a larger organisation, with various functions to do with community liaison. This further departure emerged partly from the experience and the success of the bureaux. The officers of the bureaux made contacts within each local community, in ways already indicated. It became obvious that there was further work to be done, especially in relation to school (a separate plan for which had already been developing), the Social Services Departments, and various groupings within the community, especially minorities. All these different, but related, functions were consolidated under the Community Liaison Officer.

This has had useful and hopeful effects. The police view of the problems, always detailed, has been sensitised. In many ways they have been able to harmonise programmes in this field and become much more responsive to the needs of an area or a community than in the past. This two-way exchange of information was partly implicit in the 1969 Act, but the developments have taken it beyond the strict requirements of the law into an area which seems to be fruitful and promising for the future.

Liaison with the schools is organised on a divisional basis, under the supervision of the Community Liaison Officer. The courts, social workers and the police have known for generations that any truancy means increased danger for any child in terms of likely offences. Poor school attendance is an index of likely trouble in the life of a youngster.

The police have maintained contact with the schools in various ways for generations. They have taken part in road safety campaigns within the schools as part of their routine work. They have always tried to help with the problem of truancy, and recently, by organising truancy patrols in given areas, in conjunction with the Education Authority, they have been very successful in getting a number of children off the streets and back into school.

In some of the problem areas the police stop and question all youngsters of school age who are not in school on a day when school is open. If they are not satisfied with the account the youngsters give, they either take them along to the police station where they summon the parents and the educational welfare officer or a teacher, depending upon local arrangements, and, in some instances, actually return the children to the school, if the head-teacher agrees.

This has had a marked effect on the rate of truancy in certain areas; from the police point of view it has had the additional benefit that, after such a sweep, the incidence of petty crime drops dramatically in an area. This form of co-operation is to the benefit of everyone; its results are not dramatic to the public eye, but the method is proving effective. It is one way in which the police have moved over to positive preventive work on their own account and it is encouraging.

There is a more formal, organised contact with schools and other places of education. The police go along to every sort of establishment from Infant Schools to Colleges of Further Education; talks are given, films shown and practical demonstrations arranged. The response has been highly encouraging; the children learn something of the police, and the police, according to the latest opinion, gain a great deal of useful information.

The Metropolitan Police feel that this programme has done much to develop relations with the public generally; it is immensely important to their work to present a good image to youngsters, and they are sufficiently convinced of the benefits to see that the programme is maintained and developed. It is particularly vital that they establish understanding with young people, who are responsible for a large amount of crime.

Community Liaison extends beyond the schools, of course. It can be said to take in anything which affects the life and well-being of the community. The negative aspect of this side of the work is reflected in the remark one race relations officer made to me: 'The Community Liaison Officer is the one who comes along and says sorry when some other policemen have made bloody fools of themselves and behaved like idiots.'

There is no doubt that the work of the Community Liaison Officer in connection with race relations is very important. There are areas of London, and of other cities, which have been on the brink of serious trouble for a long time; the fact that, except in one or two rare instances, this trouble has not erupted into very serious disturbances is due, in some considerable measure, to the work of the Community Liaison Officers.

They do have to come along and pick up the pieces on occasion; they are the people to say sorry, if the word needs saying. They also have the job of explaining police procedure and attitudes to people who feel they have been wrongly treated and believe themselves to have a grievance. They will also be ready to explain the point of view of people who have suffered in this way.

Only part of their work is directly related to racial problems, however. They are actively concerned in many other areas. Where local initiatives for improving play facilities for youngsters, or seeking other improvements which tend to benefit the life of the area are launched, the police, through the Liaison Officer, are willing to become involved, wherever and whenever they are asked. Their help has often been of great importance.

The police, of course, have always had their own picture of their 'own patch'; through the work of the Community Liaison Officer they have been able to form a broader picture, with far more detail of particular developments than in the past. Their own response is likely to be better informed, and their own role is made that much more effective.

If some of these activities make the policemen seem to appear in a new guise, as a quasi-social worker, that would be wrong. The role of the police is clear and their prime functions, regulated by statute and defined by law, remain the same as before. It is important to see clearly the lines of demarcation between the police and other agencies, to avoid any confusion; the police are not in any danger of confusing the issue themselves. Their work, as they know only too well, is as much prevention of crime as detection. The Community Liaison Officers play an important part in this area of police concern.

Their involvement with Social Services Departments, social work agencies, the schools, the Youth Service and minority organisations is undertaken from their own particular standpoint. It obviously offers special challenges to the police, but, despite the difficulties, the results so far have been good; they have bene-fited the police and the public at large.

Like all departures this policy presents difficulties; these, in the main, have been overcome. The police concern is genuine, their role valid, and the result has been beneficial. It reflects a response on the part of the police to the great pressures and difficulties facing all citizens in the complex modern world.

Not all policemen are convinced of the benefits of the 1969 Act. Many of them take the view that the provisions of the Act have produced a privileged class of youngsters, who are licensed to break the law. These misgivings on the part of the police are given an airing from time to time. I will discuss them in more detail in the following chapter. But, in brief, this has been the complaint of a body of the police after every new Act regarding children and young persons. In reality it is directed less to the Act than to the way the Act is being administered at this moment.

This is in reality part of the continuous dialogue which must take place between all the agencies concerned with youngsters in conflict with the law. The most important thing is that the dialogue continue, for only in that way can progress be made.

15

What Still Needs to be Done

It was not envisaged when the 1969 Act came into effect that there would be an immediate drop in the numbers of children in trouble. What the Act sought to do was devise new methods of dealing with such children. Those who have studied the history of this sort of legislation anticipated the reverse, in fact. Whenever such legislation is introduced there is a rise in the number of children and young persons coming to the notice of police, partly because of a rise in expectation of treatment. When punishment is severe there is a reluctance to prosecute; when the stated aim is treatment, there is more ready recourse to the machinery. This has happened with every Children & Young Persons Act that has been passed. It is too easy and erroneous to lay responsibility for that on the Act itself.

The Act sought to prevent significant numbers of children coming to court and the notice of the law, through better provision within the community. There has not been time to judge the effectiveness of the Act in those terms: the damage the Act sought to deal with is long-term, and not amenable to immediate remedy. The children appearing in the courts today were growing up, and their attitudes and character being shaped, before the Act was in operation. The damage to children at risk continues because the Act is not yet working properly in the areas and ways which could do most to obviate that sort of damage.

Indeed, as has been pointed out many times, the Act itself is not yet fully operative. There is a lack of money, bricks, personnel and other resources to make the Act a reality. The Act is concerned with developing new methods of work and more specific attitudes to certain community problems; patience is needed while these methods and attitudes are tested, modified and refined.

In many senses the period from 1970 to the present has been transitional in terms of the Act; we have neither the full Act nor a consolidated view of the way the Act should be made to work.

Our aspirations may have outrun our capacity, but that does not mean that the aspirations were wrong, or ought to be abandoned.

To revert to what was before would be an admission of defeat, because the old dispensation was manifestly failing. It looked more secure because it was familiar; in fact a considerable crisis was building up, and we are now coping with that crisis while trying to devise new methods to prevent such crises in the future.

This is not an argument for any form of complacency on the part of anyone. Everyone in the field knows too well that every failure means considerable suffering, distress, loss and hardship to many people, including the children and young people involved. There is no long-term view in the life of any individual child.

It is time to assess what has been achieved and what remains to be done, especially by way of improving methods of work and providing the facilities to back those methods as speedily as possible.

The first necessity is to make the orders of the court a reality. The Supervision Order must ensure that proper supervision is given, something which, in many instances, is not happening at the moment. A Care Order must mean that the necessary care and support is available to the child or young person from the moment the order is made. It is idle to pretend that this happy state of affairs prevails in most urban areas at the moment, and while this failure is acquiesced in, the whole Act falls into disrepute.

Part of a memorandum issued by the Department of Health and Social Security in July 1972 dealt with this matter.

When a boy aged 10–14 or a girl aged 10–15 who is already the subject of a care order commits an offence, or a further offence, it lies in effect with the local authority to make any changes in care and control which this behaviour shows to be necessary; the courts, having already, by a care order, conferred on the local authority power to restrict the child's liberty to such an extent as the authority consider appropriate, can do no more if the child is charged with a further offence, since the child is not of an age for committal to a detention centre or to Borstal. Therefore, when a local authority learn that the arrangements they have made for a boy or girl of this age, already committed to care, have not prevented him or her from coming to the notice of the police in connection with an offence which

may lead to prosecution, the local authority have a particular
duty to examine those arrangements with a view to exercising
a closer form of control. The child, his parents and the police
may then be made aware of what action the authority have
taken or propose to take and that, whether or not there is a
charge, the arrangements for his care will be reviewed in the
light of his behaviour. This may also be brought out in court
if a charge is made (and this is entirely a matter for the police)
so that the magistrates are not left with the incorrect impression that further offences by the subject of a care order are
treated by the authority as matters of little account.

This is good and important advice. It overlooks the difficulty
that the local authorities are experiencing in providing proper
care and control. They are experiencing great difficulty in recruit-
ing and training staff at all levels, and this means that the development of an efficient system of dealing with court work and for
placing boys and girls committed to the care of the authority has
been slow. Even where the necessary personnel do exist, the places
for helping children in special difficulty are not available.
    The desire of local authorities to continue to treat children as
far as possible within the community requires the deployment
of properly trained staff to make Supervision Orders and Care
Orders meaningful in the life of those subject to such orders.
    Too often, because of changes of staff and transfers and new
appointments, the continuity of relationship between the youngster and the supervising officer is lacking. Because of pressure of
work, the number of times the subject and supervising officer
meet is not sufficient to give guidance and support. Very often,
in court, when the child has been brought back because he has
committed a further offence, the youngster or parents will com-
complain that they have scarcely ever seen the officer, or that a
new officer has been appointed. With all the difficulties, this is
something that should be guarded against at all times, through
team planning.
    Some children, made the subject of Care Orders, but allowed
to remain at home, regard the Care Order as no different, or even
less intrusive on their lives, than supervision. Since the intention
is to provide closer control and support, such a state of affairs is
lamentable. It may or may not be true, but this has sometimes
been the opinion of both youngsters and parents.

When treatment in the community is not working, the Social Services Departments now lack the resources to provide alternative treatment, even when they come to the view that removal from home is necessary. These difficulties have been aired earlier, but one matter is important; the Social Service Departments are still working with a pattern of provision which no longer answers their needs. It reflects a period when the immediate answer for most problem youngsters was removal from home, and the buildings themselves and their location do not match the requirements of today. Within the foreseeable future these buildings, or many of them, will have to continue in use, but the future pattern of provision should be of an entirely different kind.

If treatment is to be community-based, then provision for children who have to be removed from home must be part of the community, as it never has been in the past. The time of the large community home is over, even if numbers of them will continue in use for an interim period. Each local authority, for the future, must try to have its treatment facilities within its own boundaries, so that the children who go into them are not separated from family, school and the neighbourhood that they know.

The Act will require provision in much more flexible form, in smaller units than have prevailed in the past. In each coherent 'community area' within the boundaries of the local authority, there should be some provision for the first-aid care of the children of that 'community area'. These small homes should be the first line of provision, less specialised than reception homes, which should be the second line of provision, concentrating their resources upon those children who are likely to need more specialised help and support. The basic staffing of the small 'community area' home should be a married couple, able to make a 'home' homely. These couples should be backed by the necessary resources, and their 'home' should be part of the local community, and a place where the field social workers can get to easily, where they are welcome, and which is their particular 'home' for use in all sorts of emergencies and for any problems which emerge amongst the children they are responsible for.

Such a home would blend the experience of the residential worker and the field worker in a new way, and would offer particular advantages in that way. The children, also, would feel close to home, even if not with their family and under their own roof, accessible still to their friends and the neighbourhood with which they have been familiar. The home should be part of the resources of the local team, and the residential staff should be part of that team. Decisions as to admission could be joint decisions of the residential staff and the local team of social workers.

The more highly staffed reception homes (if we wish to stick by these descriptions) should be the second line, ready to do more intensive work and make more thorough-going assessments where it is felt necessary because of particular problems manifested by particular children. The arrangement for reports to court could be organised independently of the local homes, and would lead to much more efficient use of scarce professional resources.

The 'local community' home would cater for all types of children in need, from those whose parents are ill or injured, to those who may have passed through the courts. The decision as to placement would be that of the area team and the residential staff, as I have said, and where more specialist skill or intensive study were felt necessary, the more specialist unit could be used.

This would ensure much greater flexibility of provision, and a considerable saving of resources, through their more efficient deployment. The children needing the skills of the more highly trained staff could receive them much more speedily.

This re-deployment would help in many directions. The child needing temporary relief from difficult home circumstances, the child needing help in attending school, the child likely to get into trouble with the law, could be helped and supported, even if only for a short time, within their local community. Movement from home to 'home' would be that much simpler, and the reinstatement in the child's own home that much more rapid, and much of the trauma of separation could be avoided.

A range of small units of this kind would be much more responsive to the needs of the community and the social workers, and much more adaptable to the changing needs of the community as they emerged. In all ways this system should recommend itself —there would be more reality to the back-up of the social workers and the residential workers would be closer to the homes of the children they were caring for, and much less cut off from the mainstream of social work.

At the moment the system is wasteful of skill and human resources, and inflicts unnecessary suffering upon children. It damages their chance of reinstatement in their local community. Small residential units might even be attached to local schools, particularly to help those youngsters who experience difficulty in getting to school, and are finding difficulty in other spheres of their educational life. Work with the child and the family could be continuous at all times, and involve the field workers, the residential workers and other adults interested in a particular child and family.

Such a system would speed up the day when the more specialised provision, with its higher demands on skill and resources, would be more generally available. The provision of this more highly concentrated care would be that much more economic when the small, localised units are in operation; it would ensure a concentration of effort on those most in need.

Provision of very specialised care for a small number of highly disturbed children is one of the prime necessities of social service care, which the Act requires, and which, for the most part, is not being met at the present time. This should be the concern of the Regional Planning Committees. The fact that this provision is lacking is one of the main factors which is bringing the operation of the Act into disrepute. This small minority of disturbed youngsters are those who make continual reappearances in court, despite the fact that a Care Order has been made, because lack of provision means that they remain at home, where they are at high risk, and are likely to suffer further damage, as well as inflicting it.

When the community care provision is fully operative, and many more children are prevented from coming into court, and are less damaged in their lives, there should be a diminution of demand for residential places. That day has not yet come, nor will it come for some years. In the meantime we have to bear the burden of the interim period, with a demand for resources to make community fieldwork function properly, and a continuing pressure for residential places. The cost of maintaining residential places, while trying to steer resources into the community fieldwork militates against the effectiveness of both. Until the preventive work begins to show results, local authorities must also bear the burden of maintaining expensive residential provision, and the financial burden threatens to become intolerable.

We have the worst of both worlds at the moment. Available resources are spread too thinly over too large an area of concern, and, at the same time, while everyone is paying heed to the aspirations of the Act, the development of the necessary skills and techniques is being delayed partly because of the forms of training which social workers are being given.

Generic training, which was to provide workers able to cover the whole field of concern of the expanded Social Services Departments, has been found wanting in many areas. Generic training is good at inculcating attitudes, but less successful at imparting special skills and techniques. This fact is now widely acknowledged amongst those responsible for training, and there is a need for a basic re-thinking of training over the whole field of social work.

The skills to deal with old people, the handicapped, the sick and inadequate, and with children in trouble may have basic affinities which were used to justify generic training, but the form of that training has meant a marked falling off in skills in dealing with these different categories when they actually present themselves. Indeed different individuals do not possess similar affinities and capacities over the whole range, and social workers should be encouraged to do those things they can do best, which is a more pleasurable way of working in any field of work.

It was believed that in-service training would make good this deficiency, but the pressures on the Social Services Departments have meant that in-service training has been more honoured in the breach than in the deed.

The team-work concept was also meant to provide for a cross-section of skills and insights, which it was thought would be self-renewing, but events have moved too fast. The people who once commanded the basic skills and the special techniques have been promoted or moved on, so that there are not the numbers of people with these skills left in the field able to impart them. Formal training, despite systematic efforts, has not yet been made a reality for most social workers.

Attempts to reinforce in-service training, through systematic use of visual material and the formation of a central library of material presenting these skills, have been hindered by bureaucratic uncertainty.

The most obvious way to impart these skills and 'body out' training would have been by the use of cassette material, properly photographed and carefully worked out, extending gradually over the whole field, presenting all the best methods and practice in all the essential skills and techniques. This material would have provided the essential groundwork for good training; it would have been readily available, useful for small groups and larger ones, and particularly valuable for residential staff, while they remain divorced from the mainstream of social work (or so they feel!).

Every training officer I have spoken to, every director of social services have all agreed that this would be a most useful and powerful instrument in improving the quality of social work. The most that anyone ever did to try to realise this idea was the setting up of further study groups and committees. The whole field is bedevilled with committees which manufacture paper, and little else which is of practical value for in-service training.

There are whole series of fascinating theories about deprivation, urban neglect, the causes of delinquency, school refusal and any number of topics; there are few practical demonstrations of how to cope with an hysterical girl of fourteen who finds she is pregnant, or a truculent young man who is a potential danger; little enough practical advice on the seating in a juvenile court, the way it functions, or how to address it.

The central authorities will not take decisions; the local authorities do not feel able to go ahead on their limited budgets, and perhaps one of the most valuable instruments for bringing new muscle to social work lies neglected and ignored. At the same time the valuable skills and experience of many of the best practitioners of these skills are lost, and the young social workers are left to learn for themselves, sometimes at the expense of their clients.

But even training is secondary to the number of people available for social work. The recruitment of such people will not match the need until the money is made available to the local authorities. The central government has a heavy responsibility in this area. Part of the reorganisation of social work, and the reorganisation of local government was used to shift the financial burden from central funds to local funds, rate borne. The result has been a patchy development, lacking co-ordination.

It is arguable just how much of this burden the rates can bear; there is also the question of the willingness of different local authorities to ask its electorate to bear the strain. The benefits are long-term, and the rates rise every year. Lack of local resources is hampering many important new developments. The local authorities cannot offer the salary or career structure they would wish, if they are to carry out properly their obligations, and as a result they are failing to provide properly for numbers of different categories which are their concern, not least children in trouble.

Over the country as a whole children no longer command the priority they did when they had their own separate department. Now, with a scarcity of resources, children and young people are falling behind, and, as a result, the 1969 Act is placed in jeopardy, and a great deal of advances in other fields run the same risk.

Eventually it is a political question. Children and young persons do not have votes; their families are not likely to create significant pressure groups. Parliament willed the ends; it has failed to will the means. If, at the end of the day, savings have to be made, they should be in terms of human suffering, social distress and disruption, waste of unlived life—for this reason the resources must be made available for the Act to become fully operative.

It is a reproach to us all that it has not been done. It is unfair to the local authorities that so many new responsibilities have been passed to them without the financial means being made available for them to meet those responsibilities.

At a time when every personal service is pressing for special consideration, and great pressures are building on all public services, it is important to ensure that the aspirations of the 1969 Act are kept in the forefront of the public mind and conscience. Failure now will show itself in ten to twenty years' time, and the cost then will be incalculable. We will have allowed the cycle of deprivation to make another turn.

Yet I am fearful that the responsibility will be shrugged off. There will be further exhortation to the local authorities, a few more attacks on the social services and the social workers, more reports of indiscipline amongst young people, and further calls for reversion to a more punitive attitude, more outcry about escalating crime rates. Indignation is easier than hard thought or careful, long-term provision.

To talk of these failings and to repeat the responsibility of the social services, while aware that the Social Service Departments lack the resources to carry out their duties is hypocrisy of a sort which, even in the current climate of cynical discourse, should not be allowed to pass unremarked and unchastised.

A test of the quality of any community and the civilisation of any society is how it organises services for those who are not in the comfortable, middle majority. A whole generation of damaged children looks to the social services and central government for some assurance that the damage will not be allowed to continue—the response is a test of our collective will.

If we fail to respond with courage, imagination and compassion we have failed not only this minority—we have failed ourselves and the whole culture we claim to cherish.

Bibliography

ANDRY, R., *Delinquency and Parent Pathology*, London, Methuen, 1960.

BAGOT, J., *Juvenile Delinquency*, London, Cape, 1941.

BALBIRNIE, R., *Residential Care with Children*, Bungay, Chaucer Press, 1972.

BANKS, O., *Parity and Prestige in English Secondary Education*, London, Routledge & Kegan Paul, 1955.

BEDELL, C., *Residential Life with Children*, London, Routledge & Kegan Paul, 1970.

BERLINS, M., and WANSELL, G., *Caught in the Act*, Harmondsworth, Pelican, 1974.

BIESTEK, F., *The Casework Relationship*, London, Allen & Unwin, 1967.

BLYTH, W., *English Primary Education*, London, Routledge & Kegan Paul, 1967.

BOSS, P., *Exploration into Child Care*, London, Routledge & Kegan Paul, 1971.

BOWLBY, J., *Child Care and the Growth of Love*, Harmondsworth, Penguin, 1970.

BRILL, K., *Children, Not Cases*, London, National Children's Home.

BURBURY, BALINT and YAPP, *Introduction to Child Guidance*, London, Macmillan.

BURT, C., *The Young Delinquent*, London, University of London Press, 1925.

BURTON, L., *Vulnerable Children*, London, Routledge & Kegan Paul, 1968.

CARR SAUNDERS, MANNHEIM and RHODES, *Young Offenders*, London, Cambridge University Press, 1942.

CLARK, HALL and MORRISON, *On Children*, London, Butterworth, 1974.

CLEGG, SIR A., and MEGSON, B., *Children in Distress*, Harmondsworth, Penguin, 1970.

CLOWARD, R., and OHLIN, D., *Delinquency and Opportunity*, London, Routledge & Kegan Paul, 1961.

COHEN, A., *Delinquent Boys*, London, Routledge & Kegan Paul, 1956.

DINNAGE, R., and KELLMER PRINGLE, M., *Residential Child Care*, London, Longmans, 1964.

DONNISON, D., *The Neglected Child and the Social Services*, Manchester, Manchester University Press, 1954.

DOWNES, D., *The Delinquent Solution*, London, Routledge & Kegan Paul, 1966.

DRYSDALE, L., *Therapy in Child Care*, London, Longmans, 1968.

EAST, N., *The Adolescent Criminal*, Edinburgh, Churchill, 1942.

EGGLESTONE, S., *Social Context of the School*, London, Routledge & Kegan Paul, 1967.

ERICKSON, E., *Childhood and Society*, New York, Imago, Norton, 1963.

EYSENCK, H., *The Structure of Human Personality*, London, Methuen, 1966.

FLINT, B., *The Child and the Institution*, London, London University Press, 1967.

FORD, D., *The Deprived Child and the Community*, London, Constable, 1955.

——, *The Delinquent Child and the Community*, London, Constable, 1957.

FORDER, A. (Ed.), *Social Services in England and Wales*, London, Routledge & Kegan Paul, 1969.

GIBBENS, T., and AHRENFELDT, R. H., *Cultural Factors in Delinquency*, London, Tavistock Press, 1966.

GLUECK, S., and GLUECK, E., *Unravelling Juvenile Delinquency*, Harvard University Press, 1950.

GOULD, L. (Ed.), *The Prevention of Damaging Stress in Children*, Edinburgh, Churchill, 1968.

GRUNHUT, H., *Juvenile Offenders before Courts*, London, University of Oxford Press, 1956.

HARGREAVES, D., *Social Relations in a Secondary School*, London, Routledge & Kegan Paul, 1967.

HART, T., *A Walk with Alan*, London, Quartet Books, 1973.

HEALY, W., *The Individual Delinquent*, London, Heinemann, 1915.

HEALY, W., and BRONNER, A., *A New Light on Delinquency*, Conn, Yale University Press, 1936.

HEYWOOD, J., *Children in Care*, London, Routledge & Kegan Paul, 1965.

HOLMAN, R., *Socially Deprived Families in Britain*, London, Bedford Square Press, 1970.

JACKSON, B., *Streaming*, London, Routledge & Kegan Paul, 1964.

JACKSON, B., and MARSDEN, B., *Education and the Working Class*, London, Routledge & Kegan Paul, 1968.

KELLMER PRINGLE, M., *Deprivation and Education*, London, Longmans, 1965.

——, *The Needs of Children*, London, Hutchinson, 1974.

KING, R., RAYNES, N., and TIZARD, J., *Patterns of Residential Care*, London, Routledge & Kegan Paul, 1971.

KLEIN, M., RIVIÈRE, J., *Love, Hate and Reparation*, London, Hogarth, 1938.

LANDER, B., *Towards an Understanding of Juvenile Delinquency*, Columbia University Press, 1954.

MCCORD, W., and MCCORD, J., *The Origins of Crime*, Columbia University Press, 1959.

MANNHEIM, H., *Juvenile Delinquency in an English Middle Town*, London, Routledge & Kegan Paul, 1948.

——, *Comparative Criminology*, London, Routledge & Kegan Paul, 1960.

MAYS, J., *Growing up in the City*, Liverpool, Liverpool University Press, 1954.

——, *On the Threshold of Delinquency*, Liverpool University Press, 1959.

——(Ed.), *Juvenile Delinquency, the Family and the Social Group*, London, Longmans, 1972.

MILLER, F., COURT, S., *et al.*, *Growing up in Newcastle upon Tyne*, London, Oxford University Press, 1960.

MORRIS, T., *The Criminal Area*, London, Routledge & Kegan Paul, 1957.

MUMFORD, G., and SELWOOD, J., *A Guide to Juvenile Court Law*, London, Shaw & Sons, 1974.

PACKMAN, J., *Child Care Needs and Numbers*, London, Allen & Unwin, 1968.

PARTRIDGE, W. G. M., *Middle School*, London, Gollancz, 1966.

PIAGET, J., *The Moral Judgement of the Child*, London, Routledge & Kegan Paul, 1932.

RICHARDSON, H., *Adolescent Girls in Approved Schools*, London, Routledge & Kegan Paul, 1969.

RODGERS, B., and STEVENSON, O., *A New Portrait of Social Work*, London, Heinemann, 1973.

RUNCIMAN, W., *Relative Deprivation and Social Justice*, London, Routledge & Kegan Paul, 1966.

RUTTER, M., TIZARD, J., and WHITMORE, K., *Education, Health and Behaviour*, London, Longmans, 1970.

SCHAFFER, E., and EVELYN, B., *Child Care and the Family*, London, Bell, 1968.

SHAW, CLIFFORD and MCKAY, *Juvenile Delinquency and Urban Areas*, University of Chicago Press, 1942.

SIMEY, T., *The Concept of Love in Child Care*, London, Oxford University Press, 1961.

SPINLEY, B., *The Deprived and the Privileged*, London, Routledge & Kegan Paul, 1953.

SPROTT, W., JEPHCOTT, A., and CARTER, M., *The Social Background of Delinquency*, Nottingham, University of Nottingham (private).

STEVENSON, O., *Someone Else's Child*, London, Routledge & Kegan Paul, 1965.

STORR, A., *The Integrity of the Personality*, Harmondsworth, Penguin, 1970.

STOTT, D. H., *Second Interim Report of the Glasgow Survey of Boys Put on Probation during 1957*, University of Glasgow, 1959.

TITMUSS, R., *Income Distribution and Social Change*, London, Allen & Unwin, 1962.

TIMMS, N., *Casework in the Child Care Service*, London, Butterworth, 1969.

TIZARD, J., *Community Services for the Mentally Handicapped*, London, Oxford University Press, 1957.

VENESS, T., *School Leavers*, London, Methuen, 1962.

WATSON, J., *The Child, the Court and the Magistrate*.

WHYTE, W., *Streetcorner Society*, University of Chicago Press, 1943.

WILKINS, L., *Delinquent Generations*, London, H.M.S.O., 1960.

WILLMOTT, P., *Adolescent Boys in East London*, London, Routledge & Kegan Paul, 1966.

WILLMOTT, P., and YOUNG, M., *Family Kinship in East London*, London, Routledge & Kegan Paul, 1965.

——, *Family and Class in a London Suburb*, London, Routledge & Kegan Paul, 1968.

WINNICOTT, C., *Child Care and Social Work*, Codicote Press, 1964.

WINNICOTT, D., *The Child and the Family*, London, Tavistock Publications, 1957.

——, *The Family and Individual Development*, London, Tavistock Publications, 1965.

WOOTTON, B., *Social Science and Social Pathology*, London, Allen & Unwin, 1959.

YOUNG, M., and ASHTON, E., *British Social Work in the Nineteenth Century*, London, Routledge & Kegan Paul, 1963.

YOUNG, M., and MCGEENEY, P., *Learning Begins at Home*, London, Routledge & Kegan Paul, 1969.

Index

absconders, 96–7, 99–100; *see also* truancy
activities, interest-orientated, 117–118, 119, 121–7, 130, 134–42, 143, 145, 147, 148–51
age of criminal responsibility, 19–20, 21, 23, 24, 37
alcoholism *see* drink problems
animals, sympathy for, 139, 151
Approved School Orders, 26, 34, 67, 69, 70, 71, 75, 96
approved schools, 26, 28, 34, 67, 69, 96; *see also* community homes
Asian immigrants, 161, 165
Assessment Centres, 97, 98
Attendance Centre Orders, 27, 64, 71

behaviour, disturbed, 12, 67, 69, 72, 74, 83, 122–6, 173; influences on, 12, 13, 22, 25, 53–60, 102–3, 105, 107, 109, 112, 172
binding over, 27, 64
'Blind Beak, The', 18
Borstal training, 20, 68, 71–2, 73, 75, 96, 120, 179

camps, 134–9, 141
Care Orders, 26, 27, 28, 55, 64, 65, 66–76, 95, 99, 101, 179–80, 183
care proceedings, 24–9, 37, 38, 47–50, 66–76, 169
Carpenter, Mary, 18–19
cautioning, 25–6, 170, 172, 173, 174
charitable organisations, 19, 93
The Child, the Family and the Young Offender (White paper), *1965*, 14
children, 'beyond control', 23, 24, 38; disturbed and difficult, 12, 23, 67, 69, 92–101, 102–12, 113–27, 128–42, 180–3, 186–7; educationally subnormal, 104; exploita-

tion of, 100; ill-treatment of, 24, 38, 47–50; *see also* offenders
Children Act, 1908, 19, 20
Children and Young Persons Act, 1933, 12, 13, 20–1, 22
Children and Young Persons Act, 1963, 22–3, 32, 113
Children and Young Persons Act, 1969, 11, 12, 13, 14, 17, 21, 22–9, 30–35, 51, 64–76, 82, 89, 95, 96, 113, 152, 169, 170, 177, 178–87
Children in Trouble (White paper), *1968*, 12–13, 14, 17, 169–70
Children's Departments *see* local authorities, Children's Departments
Clerkenwell prison, 18
clerks of court, 39, 40, 41, 43, 45–6, 61, 62, 81
clubs, special interest, 119, 121–7, 130, 147, 150–1
community, immigrants in the, 162; influence of on behaviour, 12, 22, 102, 103, 112; involvement in the, 113–27, 128–42, 143–54; treatment within the, 11, 12–13, 114–27, 132–3, 178–83
community areas, 181–3
community homes, 26, 29, 54–5, 69–73, 96–8, 114, 181; *see also* approved schools
community liaison, 174–7
Community Liaison Officers, 172, 174–7
Community Relations Commission, 161
community relations schemes, 145
community service, 146–7
Community Service Orders, 146
community work, 91–2, 183
compensation for offences, 14–15, 27, 28, 64